# ANTIDOTE FOR MADNESS

*by*

*Wylie Young*

*What every grammar school student should know and understand*
*but*
*which very few of our best educated people*
*either know or understand*

ROBERT SCHALKENBACH FOUNDATION
5 East 44th Street New York, N.Y. 10017

Library of Congress Catalog Card No.: 75-36898
ISBN No. 0-911312-55-2

Manufactured in the United States of America

# Dedication

We dedicate this book gratefully to the late Gilbert S. Tucker who spent most of his life trying to make clear to his fellow Americans the most fundamental and basic concepts upon which any common sense understanding of economics must be grounded. Had those who are responsible for the taxing processes in the cities of America known, understood and acted upon the principles which he explained clearly in his various books, the great cities of America would not be in such a precarious state as they now are. The first paragraph of his book, *The Self-supporting City* is as follows:

> **The City Throws Away Its Investments,**
> **Resorts to Taxation, and Goes on the Rocks**
>
> Municipal taxation as now levied can and should be a thing of the past: the American city can be a self-supporting corporation, meeting its expenses from its rightful income. Taxation is unnecessary, because the city has, in its physical properties, acquired through the years, by the expenditure of its people's moneys, a huge capital investment from which it collects only a very small part of the return earned. In streets, pavements, water supply, sewers, transit facilities, parks, playgrounds, schools and libraries; in equipment of the protective services of police, fire and sanitation, and in a hundred things, it has invested much. Little of the interest which this investment might earn finds its way back into the municipal treasury, and a large part of the value is destroyed by a system which prevents utilization of the benefits. Where would a business stand were its capital investment to earn nothing, leaving it dependent upon assessments against the owners? Of course city finances are headed for the rocks.

His book was published in 1958 by the Schalkenbach Foundation of New York.

## IN APPRECIATION

We wish to express appreciation to three persons whose suggestions and comments have been helpful in the preparation of this book: Dr. Clarence R. Thayer of New Wilmington, Pa. as our trusted grammarian; Mitchell S. Lurio of Boston as our chief counselor in matters of doctrine and Dorothy Sara of New York whose suggestions regarding technical matters that every author ought to know was helpful in the proper preparation of the manuscript. We might also mention those long periods of silence endured by my wife as she went about her duties in other parts of the house as "genius" struggled away, occasionally checking portions of the material and giving her opinion as to whether or not they were readable.

John Garver of Washington, D.C., a devoted churchman and a dedicated supporter of the ideas presented in the book has been extremely helpful, as has Mitchell Lurio, in the preparation of the revised second edition. They have given so much time that one would be justified in saying the book is the product of three minds. Their dedication to a great idea is characteristic of a great company of people across this country.

# Introduction

Whatever is happening to our world? This is the troubled query, sometimes expressed in words, but more often in puzzled looks with heads shaking in unbelieving incredulity. Why is the world-wide psyche so racked with the pains of protest and disruption? Why are so many behaving as if some form of madness had seized them in the night?

Surely, the affairs of this world are getting completely and needlessly out of hand. Madness has engulfed us all—a madness that has tainted all our thinking and affected every human institution.

Look at us,—here in America. We have always thought of ourselves as the hope of the world! Travelers, returning to their beloved America so often say, "Ours is by far the best country in the world. What a relief to be back again and to think of this as home."

But, take a closer look. Our society,—literally falling apart; our far too highly rated economy,—continually confronted with crises; all of us—shocked and baffled by vandalism, hi-jackings, murders, rapes, and robberies so that many are afraid to walk the streets at night; city fathers,—paralyzed by a what-can-we-do-now attitude toward their cities in decay; our young people,—confronted with such an array of unresolvable (or so they are led to believe) problems that they are growing cynical, becoming ripe prey for a what-the-hell attitude which expresses itself in their turning to the escape hatches of drugs, free sex, or a near pathological passion for sports. Waves of rebellion are sweeping over us; strikes by teachers,—themselves unable to recommend viable solutions; police and firemen,—threatening to walk away unless society meets their terms; great cities,—caught in violent paroxysms of protest over the attempts to deal with segregation by busing children off to distant schools.

All this, and much more! What next? Who knows?

Surely it has nothing to do with injustice,—or does it? Certainly injustice and exploitation have been with us for centuries. If these were the only causes, why are all the maddening things that shock us happening now, so late in time? A new ingredient must have been added for no sensible observer could leap to the conclusion that world-wide injustices have had nothing to do with the current rash of human misbehavior and seething rebellion. Injustice may not be new and regimes of former days may have practiced more blatant forms of injustice than we ever dream of today, but, in dealing with this problem, we cannot afford to discount the significance of injustice and its inevitable consequences,—"gross inequity."

Our world today is different than it has ever been in all history. To put it bluntly, America has happened to it! Because we became the quick inheritors of a vast stretch of arable and mineral laden land, and because millions of Americans came to experience the thrill of having easy access to all kinds of useful land, we became the jolting instigators of change. Had it not been for the discovery of the Western Hemisphere masses of Europeans would still be imprisoned by such an array of entrenched injustices as would make the thoughtful historian shudder in his books.

Try this idea on for size. Two hundred years ago missionaries of the church and emissaries of industry and commerce fanned out across the world, the former to save souls and the latter to make deals. In those countries where misery and poverty had been a way of life for millions, those afflicted never questioned the unavoidableness of their lot. They were completely docile. It never seemed to occur to them that things could or should be different.

But that was before the multiple ways of increased communication had opened the eyes of the oppressed so that they could compare their ways of living with the ways in other lands. Now, the huddled masses in many lands are no longer docile. They can see the fruits of inequity all about them and seeing and knowing has made them restless.

This book is written to point the way to a proper, peace-engendering antidote for the madness that has gripped our world, a madness that was latent in the traditional forms of injustice, but which are now coupled with a deepening conviction that docility is no longer appropriate. In our own country, many,—especially among the unprincipled and frustrated—not having a very strong grip on the verities of life, and not knowing where all the trouble is coming from, react negatively and strike back with antisocial behavior and acts of criminal violence. Those who are built of sterner stuff still "hang in there," hoping against hope that somehow we can bring it all together. There is a logical explanation for all this, and there is a way to deal with the madness of our times.

# Foreword

As a college professor I can testify that the sub-title of *Antidote for Madness*—"What every high school student should know but which very few of our best educated people either know or understand"—is not an exaggeration. Many readers of this book will be amazed and disturbed upon realizing the significance of the basic facts revealed. A great majority of well-read people may well suffer a sense of shock, disbelief and disorientation upon reading the first few chapters. Economic pressures which create bad social conditions are carefully explained with a clarity seldom achieved by most modern writers, for the simple reason that they could not themselves answer certain questions. Perhaps you will have better success than most of my students have in their attempts to answer the following questions:

1. When some *physical* item is used as a tax base, is the tax automatically passed on to the user or consumer?
2. Can you name any item or items which, when taxed, the tax is *not* passed on or shifted?
3. Would it make any difference in the selling price of any such item if the tax was or was not passed on?
4. Have you heard about incentive taxation and do you know how it works?
5. Are you familiar with the law of rent as discovered some 200 years ago by the English economist, David Ricardo?
6. Can you give a formal statement of the law or even explain in the most general terms how the law operates?

All of these questions are crucial and in my classes I keep insisting that, without knowing the answers, concerned citizens will never be able to resolve the plethora of problems that confront our society today.

Approach this book with an open mind, and it is likely to change your entire social philosophy. There are very few books for which I would care to make that claim.

**Steven B. Cord**
**Professor, Division of Social Sciences**
Indiana University of Pennsylvania
Indiana, Pennsylvania.

# Contents

CHAPTER ONE

# A Cornerstone of Truth

A strange myth is abroad in the land. Most people have come to believe that economics, in and of itself, is hopelessly complicated. A cartoon in *The New Republic* shows a torrid jungle scene with two characters labled "economic advisors" leading the President by the hands. All three are walking unknowingly on the back of a huge alligator. The President is saying, "I hope you guys know where you are going!" It is a timely shot at the confusion that characterizes so many of those whose business it is to comprehend what to many begins to look like the incomprehensible.

A recent editorial in The New York Times says, "The numbers illustrating unemployment, inflation, crime, trade deficit and other problems are frightening . . . but what makes them catastrophic is that nobody understands them and nobody knows what to do." This is the understatement of the century. It may have been true one hundred years ago, but today there are those who know exactly what is wrong and exactly what to do. The trouble is that it is almost impossible to get the children of this age who have been sociologically conditioned to accept the unacceptable to understand where it was that we all went wrong. We have all been so badly misled and misinformed that even the majority of our most highly educated people are inclined to agree that "nobody understands."

In all candor, those who do understand represent the most frustrated and baffled group of people extant. Many, viewing the situation as a challenge, never stop trying to share their insights, but they never cease to be amazed at the incredulity with which their explanations are met. Many, confronted with such universal myopia, finally give up and say, "What's the use?" As for us, having been one of the dogged former class, we are going to make one last, desperate effort. Perhaps the very peril of our current predicament will help us get our message over, for the madness of this age is everywhere apparent. Even those who have been most thoroughly conditioned should be able to see the extreme gravity of our present situation.

Many people believe that economics is too complicated and beyond their comprehension. It is not. With the entire business world believing and acting as if false theories are true, the resulting superstructure can indeed make it seem beyond the comprehension of ordinary people. We admit that economics appears complicated, but only because business practices violate basic economic laws. It is impossible to build a society on errors and fallacious policies. Sooner or later it will turn into a house of cards. Pure economics is not complicated at all, nor is it theoretically impossible to correct our present system, even though it is too far over the hill for easy or quick relief. Many strengths have been built into it and there is no need to wipe the slate clean and to start all over again with all basic processes completely changed.

An economic system that is properly based need not appear complicated. There is a mysteriously wonderful computer-like instrument that we call the free market which, if allowed to do its work unhindered, will automatically cause human beings to function as if they themselves were almost omniscient. If the system is properly based, there will be checks and balances such as the modern man just wouldn't believe.

If you want to stand a new lead pencil on end and have it hold its position without any support, the essentials are that the surface be level and the base of the pencil be plumb. If the base of the pencil has even a slight slant, guy wires and buttresses of sorts will be necessary. The same is true of an economy. If there is one basic flaw in the process where injustice invariably occurs so that one individual or group is favored at the expense of all others involved, guywire types of devices or artificial buttresses of sorts will have to be introduced to compensate. Our system today is so replete with such props that "hopelessly complicated" are the words that most accurately describe our situation.

2

When an urgent need to understand a condition arises those who have the ability to ask the right questions are more likely to come up with the proper answers. Anyone who is concerned about our socio-economic problems but who does not have the wit to ask why so few have so much and so many have so little, may as well turn his attention to other matters. If our established system seems to have a built-in tendency toward inequity, wise people will try to analyze the process to discover at what point or points inequity appears. Far too many will blame it all on human greed and proceed to resolve the issue with pious attitudes and moralizations. This has been the conventional religious approach. Because religious leaders have refused to admit there is any other reason, they have been retreating from the arena of reality and so, providing very little direction in the real search.

One highly original philosopher put the question this way: Why is it that as a society "advances in the scale of material progress—just as closer settlement and more intimate connection with the rest of the world, and greater utilization of labor-saving machinery, make possible greater economies in production and exchange, and wealth in consequence increases, not merely in the aggregate, but in proportion to population—so does poverty take a darker aspect. Some get an infinitely better and easier living, but others find it hard to get a living at all . . . . This association of poverty with progress is the great enigma of our times."

Now, without further comment, let us get down to brass tacks by stating as forcefully as possible that unless, and until, we understand where and how inequity is allowed to become integral in the economic process of production and exchange we will go from bad to worse; the worst being some brand of fascist dictatorship. If that comes all our hopes for freedom will have vanished and future celebrations of our independence will have been made impossible.

Our "corner-stone of truth" has to do with a basic principle of taxation. Most people assume that the sole purpose of taxation is to pay for the many services that government provides. We all want security both in the world and in the streets. We want schools, roads, sewers, sanitary controls, fire protection and all the varied contributions to social life that a well administered system of government can provide. Taxation, therefore, is accepted as inevitable and necessary. But taxes can also serve as a means of establising and maintaining a state of equity and elemental justice. However, this is beyond the knowledge of most people. The most powerful and influential people perpetuate this ignorance. If the average citizen, educated or otherwise, can be kept in the dark about the potential power of a particular tax policy to establish and maintain equitable conditions and simple justice, these upper class people will do everything in their power to keep blinders on the eyes of the people. By keeping the remedy under wraps they will have denied millions their just rewards, and they will have destroyed any hope Americans might have had to become a source of enlightment to the rest of the world. The pity of it is that this remedy was clearly set before the nation one hundred years ago. It won thousands of enthusiastic supporters but it also 'roused the ire of those who had been profiting unduly by their "vested injustice," and caused them to set into motion a propaganda effort which succeeded in relegating the idea to the rejected accumulation of discredited and ridiculed proposals.

Those who for selfish reasons have assiduously conducted a campaign of ideological sabotage, have done inestimable damage to this country and, indirectly, to the entire world. It is not mere conjecture, on the part of those of us who understand how public revenue should be raised, to declare that we Americans have no other choice but to face up to our failure to understand. Unless we do correct our lack of understanding and act accordingly we can expect to continue the gradual decline which has already set in, or perhaps be confronted with sudden ruin.

## 3

Almost everyone realizes that our country is ripe for some kind of tax reform. Most thoughtful people believe that we could find better kinds of tax levies, but this being so, how many of your favorite writers have been recommending *specific* new tax sources? Have you read anywhere that there is a vast and virtually untapped tax source? Probably not.

Most writers in economics got their education in the colleges and were never properly instructed about taxation. There is a great hue and cry in their ranks about our real estate taxes. Many are saying, "They are too high; they are killing us; perhaps we should get rid of property taxes altogether." Like a broken record this comment keeps coming with its dismal repetition. Do you know why this is a totally unacceptable proposal?

Every once in a while some presumably knowledgeable commentator allows his picture to be broadcast while he says, "Our schools are in real danger; no longer can we hope to support them with the real estate tax. We must find some other tax source, whereby our schools could be administered without hurting most of our property owners." Ah! That is just what this country needs,—someone besides ourselves to pay our taxes! However, if he thinks there is such a tax source that might be used to put our schools on the corner of Sound and Secure Avenues, why does he not identify it? I listened to one teacher pontificating in this matter but just when it seemed that he was about to name the source he shrugged his shoulders and said, "That is a problem for our legislators." All we can say is that they had better know more than he does!

An overlooked tax source does exist in super-abundance. Its usefulness as such was thoroughly documented by our (so far) unnamed philosopher-economist. Despite the fact that his writings were published in more languages than those of any other economist in the world, we would guess that less than one percent of the American people could even guess who he was. We have already tossed out a few broad hints as to his identity. That so few people even know the barest outlines of his proposals is one of the tragedies of our times, and represents one of the most colossal cover-ups in all history. Not everyone who has helped to perpetuate this cover-up acted with deliberate intent to deceive. One cannot say as much for many very wealthy people who were either blinded by their own greed or chose to lie and misrepresent the facts deliberately. If their greed had blinded them, they probably imagined that they were justified in meeting truth with bald-faced denials and frightening predictions. In any case, because of their enormous influence their very strong opinions were not challenged by the educators who merely took the line of least resistance, not realizing how devastating their own indifferent attitude would prove to be.

## 4

Assuming that you, the reader, have had some exposure to economics in school, let us test your knowledge and see if you can identify the tax source which I say exists. If, because of our preliminary remarks, you do suspect what it is, have you ever tried to figure how a tax on this source might be instituted? If all this is Greek to you, it is my contention that you, along with millions of others, have been "had." It is also my contention that the great majority of people have been misled and confused in their understanding of some of the most elemental aspects of economic and social life.

In their desperate search for new tax sources some states have passed what are known as "tax anything" laws. The legislators do not even know enough to be ashamed of themselves. Hence the plethora of sales taxes that have been spawned in cities, counties and states. Everyone seems to know that sales taxes are bad. It is no secret that they penalize and bear most heavily upon the poor but it is seldom pointed out that they also penalize the rich. All in all, sales taxes are a stupid answer to the need for revenue. Nevertheless, the state of general ignorance being what it is, we have all heard the old cliche, "And five cents for the Governor, please." With a helpless feeling of resignation we pay up and walk out.

You have often heard it said that a tax, any tax at all, is always passed on to the ultimate consumer. Based upon your present understanding are you in a position to affirm or deny this allegation? Are you one of those who have a gut feeling that the moment something is adopted as a tax base, that particular something is going to be more expensive and more difficult to acquire? Did you ever consider that the reason this seems to be true is that most of our taxes are of such a character that the tax is indeed passed on to the consumer? Did you ever wonder if there might be a tax source, from which the tax was *not* passed on, so that the tax would not make the item more expensive? Would you believe that there might be a tax source which, simply because it was being taxed, would be cheaper to buy than if it were not taxed?

If you never had this proposition put before you, and if no one ever explained that there is something which, when taxed, is actually made cheaper, and so is made more readily available to those who might want to use it, you can attribute your ignorance to the aforementioned cover-up. However, you are no different than the great majority of educated people whose knowledge of such matters has been either intentionally or inadvertently restricted. The cover-up has been so effective that many highly placed and responsible people in all walks of life attempt to deal with socio-economic problems without ever mentioning what is actually causing most of our difficulties.

Let us now move closer to our presumed "magic" tax source. If you have not guessed, or if no one has told you what this book is all about, you will be needing more than vague hints. Therefore, (and here comes the give-away) when we say that it, and it alone, is the source of all wealth, and that everyone is eager to secure as much of this item as possible, we are sure the secret is out. Yes, it is *land*. Moreover, it is time to state dogmatically that any tax that is levied on anything except land (or as we should always say, "land value") is always passed on to the ultimate consumer, but a tax on land value is never passed on, or as the economists would say, "cannot be shifted." Having made this statement we must emphasize that anyone who does not understand this cannot deal intelligently with the issues that confuse and baffle so many.

Here then, is an important assertion. You should have it constantly before you as we proceed. Taxes that are based upon anything that has been produced by human labor are *always* passed on to the ultimate consumer. Every economist knows this to be a fact. It is virtually an economic axiom. The inescapable tendency is for such a tax to increase the consumer cost of the item taxed, to limit the quantity that might be produced and eventually to impair its quality. Unfortunately, most of the taxes we pay are based upon labor products, labor itself (incomes) or the right to sell the things we make (sales). This latter is the most outrageous ploy of all.

On the contrary, a tax that is based upon land value *cannot* be passed on, either to the renter or the buyer of land. This assertion is usually made in all economics textbooks, but little or nothing is ever made of it. Yet, here is the crux of our socio-economic problem. Any careful effort to put this well-established fact in its proper perspective would literally revolutionize our life-style. Every economist who is worthy of his salt will admit that a tax on land value cannot be passed on, but too many economists know that there are powerful and influential people who do not want this fact exposed, and so they are certain to get more "salt" if they play the fact down and do not follow through to its ultimate conclusions.

Nevertheless, this is the all-important formula. As the current idiom would have it—"We are laying this proposition on you," that taxes on labor products are *always* passed on, making everything except land more expensive, but taxes based upon land value are *never* passed on, making land cheaper than it otherwise would be. In saying this we are stating one of the most far-reaching and, if it were acted upon intelligently, one of the most revolutionary ideas ever promulgated.

## 4

I realize only too well that this "earth-shaking" declaration will be received by most readers in perfect calm. Why then, if you are among those who are convinced that spectacular changes are in order, are you not throwing your hat in the air and screaming "Eureka!" On the other hand, if you are quite satisfied with things pretty much as they are, why are you not filled with rage that such a statement is being made in black and white? If this is indeed that "cornerstone of truth" I promised to reveal, why are you not saying to yourself, "By Jove, I believe the man really has something!" In your present state of mind you may suspect that this principle isn't important at all, but if it really is, why does it fall on you with such a dull thud? To use another figure, why does it cause you to sail off like a lead balloon?

John Gardner of Common Cause recently said that our generation is afflicted with a kind of functional blindness, and that our trouble is not so much that we do not have the ability to solve our problems as that we are incapable of seeing what the problems are in the first place? It is certainly true that when we are faced with some difficult problem the first step toward a viable solution is to be able to put all the elements involved in proper perspective.

So we are faced with the necessity of explaining why people do not recognize the significance of the principle in the first place. Certainly not all the professors avoid its implications in a spirit of self-serving. There must be a fundamental flaw in our way of thinking. Those of us who recognize this principle as one of the most basic of all economics axioms are all too poignantly aware of how seemingly impossible it is for moderns to react either enthusiastically or with troubled apprehension. This seemingly total lack of understanding has baffled us for years.

Let us hazard a guess as to why this is so. In most economics textbooks, and therefore, in almost any dissertation on economic processes, there is seldom any distinction made between land and labor products. In many texts land is plainly referred to as wealth. Land is not wealth. It is only the *source* of wealth, and until labor applies itself to land to create or produce something that has exchange value no wealth is involved. It is little wonder that conventionally trained journalists fall into the trap of assuming that land and labor products are alike. This is the fatal error that lies at the heart of our economic system, As we go on with our story we will show how this error originated and became part of our ideology.

When two people discuss economic matters and this distinction is not clearly understood there can be no real dialogue or meeting of minds. When legislators are totally unaware of this distinction and in their ignorance try to resolve some sticky economic problem they simply cannot come up with accurate solutions. Their recommendations will be as phony as a gallon of water in a gas tank. In the past forty years they have proved their ineptitude over and over again. The strange thing is that we are still gullible enough to talk about the practicality of government controls and price fixing or the "obvious need" for the government to subsidize this or that sagging segment of the economy.

If, in our thinking, we can make a clean-cut distinction between the nature of land and the nature of labor products; if we can come to appreciate the fact that taxes on land value cannot be passed on, whereas, any and all taxes other than those on land value must be paid at the end of the line; and if we can bring into focus the many benefits to our society that would accrue should we make a shift in our tax policies, we might discover the magic key which would save us all from the madness that has engulfed us and that is slowly but surely corrupting both our business and political institutions. We cannot survive this tempo toward ruin for long. We must either come to grips with the facts or pay the penalty, and the penalty is frightful to contemplate.

CHAPTER TWO

# Two Entirely Different Entities

In order to appreciate the significance of the two closely related facts, that taxes on land value are never passed on, while taxes on buildings and improvements are always passed on by the landowner to the user or buyer, our first concern must be to point out the reasons why these are facts to be relied upon. Naturally, the one place where both of these facts come into play is in the property tax.

It has become the fashion for speakers or writers to take back-hand slaps at the property tax. Seldom does anyone impart any wisdom on the real issues involved. Never have I heard a single person, either in an important office or running for office, identify the real trouble. One gets the impression that all men in official positions have agreed never to expose the central nerve of the problem, but this suspicion has given way to the doleful realization that "they just don't understand." If someone does venture a recommendation, he usually proves that he does not realize that property taxes involve two entirely different entities, land and buildings. (We should always say "buildings and improvements," but for purposes of brevity we will usually use the one word "buildings" and imply the rest.)

Like Topsy, the property tax in America just grew. In our early days, those who were influential in establishing tax policies never suspected it would make any difference whether they taxed land or buildings, or both together. So we have traditionally levied taxes on both alike, as if they were alike, and as if taxes affected each in identical ways.

Before we can hope to have a meeting of minds, we must distinguish clearly between the nature of land and the nature of whatever improvements may have been made, either by increasing the productive capacity of the land itself or by the construction of buildings. Indeed, unless we can keep land and all types of improvements sharply separated in our thinking, there can be no clarity of thought in the entire field of economics. What then are these differences? It is a fact that land and buildings are as different as chalk and salt, and that taxes affect each in diametrically opposite ways.

| THE NATURE OF LAND | THE NATURE OF BUILDINGS |
|---|---|
| Land is God-made, the given natural resources of our environment. Properly defined, "land is the whole material universe except man and his products." Therefore, land includes forests, lakes, rivers, oceans, the air we breath and all natural forces and manifestations. | Buildings are man-made. They are products of human labor and represent a form of wealth. Properly defined, wealth is "any material thing produced by labor from land and having exchange value." A building can be both wealth and capital, depending upon its use. |

Now read the column on the right.

---

| | |
|---|---|
| Land is in limited supply. There is just so much and no more. It can neither be created nor destroyed. No one can manufacture farms, create mines or fabricate a new world. Land is plentiful but not all land is valuable. | Buildings are in limitless supply. If not prevented or if conditions are right we can add any number of buildings we want or need. Buildings are constantly being constructed, repaired, remodeled, replaced or destroyed. |
| Land is the sole source of all wealth, but it is not wealth. We emphasize this because many economics textbooks say that it is so. To do this is to imply that land is a commodity and should be treated as such. This is to commit a grievous error in semantics and leads to hopeless confusion. | A building is wealth, though in many instances it can be both wealth and capital. A house, lived in by its owner is wealth. If it is being rented to residential tenants, or to manufacturers or to store managers it is capital. Any wealth being used to produce more wealth is capital. |
| Land will sometimes increase in value 1000% in a short time. Discovery of some natural deposit or news of a proposed bridge or highway will cause striking increases in value. Such enormous increases are the result of market demand for deposits and/or for the use of advantageous locations. | No building ever increases 1000% in value. Buildings, if destroyed, can be replaced. The chief consideration is reproduction cost. Labor and materials may have doubled or tripled but a 1000% increase in reproduction costs could never occur except under runaway and uncontrolled inflation. |

Land values increase as community services are made available. Police and fire protection; telephone, water, gas and electric services; churches, libraries, schools, hospitals and character building institutions all tend to increase land values. These are socially created services and their presence in the community causes increases in land values.

Building values are not affected by the multiplicity of community services available. Socially-created services that vastly improve the life style of area residents never affect the price of buildings. Reproduction costs and depreciation factors are the major considerations. The citation of a building as an historical landmark might add to its value but this rarely occurs.

---

Land worth or value is determined by a process of open market bidding. Land is worth the most that anyone at any time is willing to pay for rent or purchase. If no bids are being made, a research study of land sales in the surrounding area will serve as a useful guide.

Building values are ascertained by fairly reliable calculations, taking into account reproduction costs and standard obsolescence factors. Bids may be affected if a building is designed to meet a particular need or if alterations will be needed for the intended use.

---

*Rent* is paid for the use of land or landsites. Any increase in the tax on land value does not affect the rent payment. It does decrease the rent-take by the landowner. If the state takes 10% of the annual rent in taxes the landowner keeps 90%. If the state takes 90% the landowner keeps 10%. He cannot add to the rent to recoup the tax because he is already getting as much as the market allows. If a higher tax on land value is levied the tax on buildings should be proportionately reduced. Most of the people who own land and who use their land would benefit.

*Interest* is paid for the use of buildings. We mistakenly refer to it as rent. Inasmuch as all taxes levied on labor products will be passed on, the building owner must pay the tax if he is using the building. If he rents or sells, the user or buyer must pay. A tax levy of from 2% to 5% of the annual interest earning of the building must be paid by the user and this automatically reduces the annual earning capacity of the investment. Owners, if renting, can pass the tax on; but whether paid by owner or renter, it is the user who pays in the end.

---

A tax on land value is never punitive. It is a payment in lieu of rent. All land that is worth using calls for a rent commensurate with its value. If the rent is paid to the state as a tax, the private landowner may feel punished; but upon thinking it through, he will realize that the government is forbidding him to take what is not rightfully his. This is a legitimate function of government.

A tax on buildings is always punitive. It is an arbitrary "fine" imposed by the state and constitutes an annually collected penalty for producing or buying something of value. Such a policy is contrary to the fundamental purpose of government which should encourage and not penalize citizens for creating wealth. Every penny of taxation on buildings makes buildings more expensive.

---

Taxes on land value should never exceed the annual rental value of land or even be so high as to impair the incentive to own land or to make land deals. Landowners, as such, may do no work, but understanding and good judgment are important. For exercising such, recompense is due. If land value taxes are increased beyond a certain point, there might be no profit at all in buying or selling land. Landowners should receive reasonable remuneration; but with the risk factor removed there would be no excessive gain nor crippling loss.

Taxes on buildings should never even approach the point where the tax is so high as to impair the incentives for investment building. All over America private enterprise is being shackled because taxes are taking too much of the annual investment earning of capital. It is absurd to assume that there is enough tax money to replace all the outworn buildings, either in cities or in the country districts. By taxing land value to its full potential and taking taxes off buildings, the price of both land and buildings would be greatly reduced.

In commenting upon these basic differences let us summarize their significance:

Whereas: land is the natural God-given source of all wealth, having required no expenditure of either capital or labor; and conversely, buildings are man-made and cannot be produced without the expenditure of labor and capital—

Whereas: land values increase, due to population pressure and increased demand for raw materials, sometimes advancing thousands of percentage points beyond what they once were; and conversely, building values never increase as a result of population pressure or increased social demands upon materials, but rather are determined by obsolescence factors and reproduction costs—

Whereas: land, when taxed, becomes less expensive to buy; and conversely, buildings, when taxed, become more expensive both to build and to maintain (raw materials must be secured from high priced land, and higher taxes are necessarily paid by the user)—

Whereas: a low tax on land value makes land more expensive to buy; and conversely, a low tax on buildings, when coupled with a high tax on land value, makes buildings cheaper, both to build and maintain—

Whereas: a high tax on land value does not impair the productive capacity of land; and conversely, a high tax on buildings will result, sometimes in the razing of a building to escape the tax, but more often, in creating conditions that make the construction of buildings unprofitable, thus adding to decay and obsolescence in a city—

Whereas: all of the above is true, and it is customary to conclude such a list of "reasons why" with a solemn "let us therefore, firmly resolve," our present state of ignorance regarding property taxes prompts us to change the usual phrase to "let us, therefore, try to understand."

Let us, therefore, try to understand that: 1) it is unscientific to tax land and buildings alike; 2) any tax based upon the value of buildings and improvements will penalize builders and do-ers and thus discourage the whole building process; 3) theoretically, the only tax that can be justified is a tax based upon land value.

In our next chapter we will be explaining why the basic difference between land and labor products calls for and demands, in the name of justice, a tax policy that takes these differences into account. The suggestion that we levy a heavier tax on land value and a lighter tax on buildings and improvements will strike most people as an invitation to disaster. We all instinctively realize the importance of land and we certainly do not wish to make it more difficult to come by. But that is exactly what our present tax policy does to us. Because we have always taxed more heavily the things we produce, making them more expensive, we quite illogically leap to the conclusion that if we tax land value any more it is bound to make land more expensive both to buy and to rent. In fact, the exact opposite is true.

CHAPTER THREE

# Diametrically Opposite Effects

The foregoing, therefore, are the major differences between land and labor products. In itemizing these differences we have provided all the facts one might need to reach certain important conclusions. It is as if we had placed all the pieces of a jigsaw puzzle on a table and said, "Now, put the picture together." In the previous chapter, we declared that all reputable economists agree that taxes on land value cannot be shifted or passed on. In this we appealed to authority for truth. Now we are ready to appeal to truth for authority. With these facts before us we can logically deduce that: 1) taxes on land value cannot be shifted but must be borne by the landowner; 2) any increase in the tax on land value will result in the reduction of the price of whatever land is so taxed; 3) taxes on any labor product, from needles to skyscrapers, are always passed on to the ultimate consumer; and 4) our custom of taxing any and all labor products tends to increase the price of everything we need and must buy.

## (1) WHY IS IT THAT TAXES ON LAND VALUE CANNOT BE SHIFTED?

First, there is just so much land. The supply is fixed and no one can manufacture any more. Since land is the source of all wealth there is a constantly changing market for its use. Competition for its use is relative but the keener the competition the higher the value.

Second, if a piece of land has any value at all, the price or rent will be determined by the most that anyone might pay for whatever that particular land might provide. Farm land is scaled according to its fertility and accessibility to markets and paid for at so much per acre. Commercial sites in cities are scaled according to location and paid for at so much per front foot. The price of homesites in cities depends largely upon the prevailing level of income and financial ability of those living in the area involved. There are other factors that are too obvious to mention. Land that is rich in some mineral deposit is scaled according to the market demand for whatever material is involved.

Third, men are constantly bidding for the right to use all kinds of land. For the privilege of using some land men will pay a fortune. According to Fortune Magazine* John Galbreath and Peter Ruffin, the two men who were responsible for building the Socony-Mobil building at 42nd Street and Lexington

* July 1955—p. 132.

Avenue in New York, are "thought to be paying something in excess of $500,000 a year" for the ground rent. This is to be paid for 60 years. That is one kind of land, but millions of acres in America would bring no rent at all. Landowners usually try to get the maximum that anyone is willing to pay, but there is always a limit beyond which no one will go. Therefore, just as the supply of land is fixed, so the rent of any piece of land is also fixed by the open market at any given time or place.

Inasmuch as every landowner is in competition with all other landowners this will restrict prices. Should a landowner ask more than the competition warrants, renters or buyers will go elsewhere. Land prices are not subject to the whim of the landowner. If they were, everyone except landowners would be in big trouble. It would be ridiculous for a landowner to mortgage his land and hope to pay the interest charge by raising the rent. If two persons were to own land jointly, and one insisted upon taking two-thirds of the rent, the other part-owner could not recoup by raising the rent. In actual fact, there are two part-owners of every bit of land in private use, the state and the landowner. If the state, in exercising its taxing power, were to take two-thirds of the annual rent instead of a picayune one to three percent of the total land value (selling price), the so-called landowner could do nothing about it. Perhaps we should abandon the term "landowner" and use the word "landholder" instead. That is all that those of us who own land really are.

These things being so, it should be clear that taxes on land value cannot be shifted. However, we have had almost no experience with the government ever basing the property tax on land value. All over America and Canada such taxes are based upon the combined value of land and buildings. Invariably, due to the pressure on assessors by owners of vacant and unused land, assessments on land value are very much lower than they should be when real market value is considered. This tends to make assessments on buildings relatively higher than they would be if land were assessed at full market value. Because the conventional methods prevail, rents are always increased when taxes are raised, but that is because the bulk of the tax is based on buildings. Our failure to understand why rents are raised as taxes go up is just part of the confusion that arises because we are not trained to separate land and buildings in our thinking. We should always remember that they are entirely different in character and that taxes affect each in opposite ways.

## (2) WHY WOULD AN INCREASE IN THE TAX ON LAND VALUE REDUCE THE PRICE OF LAND?

Land prices are arrived at by computing the annual rental value at 5% (20 X ARV). Inflation will distort this figure but usually a 5% return is acceptable when land is put in use by well established institutions. Let us suppose that the annual rent for a piece of land is $100.00. This is what a landowner might receive by renting merely the land and leaving all the work and worry of producing to someone else. It would be like putting so much money in a savings bank and receiving 5% annually. To receive $100.00 from a bank as interest one would have to deposit $2,000.00. Actually the simplified method of computing the selling price of land is to multiply the annual rent by 20.

An increased tax on land value reduces the *price* of land but not the *rent*, for full rent must be paid by the leaseholder to someone. Remembering that it is the landowner, as such, who collects the rent, and the capitalist, as such, who collects the interest (they are often, but not always, one and the same), when the state permits the landowner to keep all but a tiny portion of the rent the capitalist is obliged to pay almost all of the tax, if most of the tax is based upon the building. The landowner, therefore, goes almost scot-free. When the renter or user of the property finds his rent has been increased because the tax on the building has been raised he is unable to do anything about it because the capitalist (in most cases also the landowner) can escape by passing the tax on to the renter. However, going back to our $2,000 example, should the state take 50% of the annual rent, the landowner's rent-take would be $50.00 instead of $100.00, and land which previously sold for $2,000 would now sell for $1,000. Many well-educated people, upon hearing this, will be horified but they are so lacking in proper background that they will not see what a boon this would be to all who are *using* their land. The only people who would be disadvantaged would be those who are playing dog-in-the-manger with land and holding it for speculation. Their object is to hold land out of use until someone who believes in working for what he gets is willing to pay an exorbitant price for the right to use their land.

There is a law in Pennsylvania which grants permission to City Councils of the Cities of the Third Class to raise the city tax solely or differentially from a tax on land value. This would automatically eliminate or reduce the taxes on buildings and improvements. In most instances the city tax represents about 30% of the entire tax levies by the three taxing authorities, the City, School Board and County.

A sudden shift of 30% of the tax levy from a tax on land and buildings alike to a tax on land value would so increase the tax on vacant or unused land that many vacant lots would be thrown on the market. Therefore, vacant land would be sold at greatly reduced prices, so that many people would start thinking of ways of putting land to use. However, the few very influential people, who own more land than they intend to use themselves, will set up such a hue and cry that any effort to make the law operative will be resisted. The "hue and cry" usually takes the form of heavy pressure on City Council.

If Council shows signs of giving in, the pressure will be applied to editors and managers of newspapers. Despite the fact that taxes on 80% of all homeowners will be greatly reduced; that taxes on manufacturing plants will be lower; that additions and improvements to homes, stores and factories could be made without the usual penalties or fines, these far too influential owners of vacant land will usually prevail. Meanwhile, people go on paying exorbitant prices for land and exorbitant taxes on buildings. As we have said again and again, even the best educated people "do not understand." They know all about "the birds and the bees" but no one ever explained to them the first thing about taxation!

As a matter of fact, most landowners would find themselves in a highly advantageous position. By investing capital and improving their land, instead of making money by the negative and unproductive process of land speculation, they would be making a positive contribution to the community. As many citizens became aware of the new opportunities to build, a veritable flood of new prospects for land sales would develop. Let real estate agents consider that opportunities for sales would greatly increase and that commissions lost because of the decrease in land prices would be more than made up for by commissions on the finer buildings that would be constructed on a tax-exempt basis.

In basic theory (2) we just knocked the bottom out of the price of land! Be assured that unless you have thousands of acres of land which you do not intend to use, or dozens of vacant city lots which you do not intend to develop, this is "gospel" or good news. Do not for one moment allow the suspicion to nag you that by having the government levy higher taxes on land value, and in doing so reduce land prices, the economy will go into a tail-spin. Quite the contrary, it will leap forward and we will all be swept up with it to enjoy its many benefits.

## (3) WHY ARE TAXES ON LABOR PRODUCTS ALWAYS PASSED ON TO THE ULTIMATE CONSUMER?

Here again we encounter the most important difference between land and labor products. No one produces land. It is here and has been for eons past. It is the God-given factor in the process of wealth production. Though abundant in extent and amazingly rich in the variety and quantity of its supplies and powers, when economic considerations prevail there are sharp limits to its gifts.

On the contrary there is no limit to the number of things that can be produced by labor when it has proper access to land and its resources. Of prime importance is the fact that the production of any commodity is within the volition of the individual. The fact that the potential supply of commodities is unlimited brings into play an entirely different set of influences than those which make it impossible for landowners to shift the tax on land values.

It is the *cost of production* which is the basic consideration in determining the price of a labor product. If any item can be sold at a price which will cover the costs and bring an adequate profit, well and good. If costs are higher than people are willing to pay, production will cease. Manufacturing concerns all have cost accountants who carefully check all expenses involved. Of the many cost factors, taxes are highly significant, and these are lumped together and added to all the other costs. As each stage of production is completed all taxes (except those on land values) are reflected in the ultimate price paid by consumers.

### (4) WHY DO TAXES ON LABOR PRODUCTS INCREASE THE PRICES OF ALL COMMODITIES?

We have almost answered the above question in the preceding section. Any and all costs, including taxes, must be included in the price to the consumer. When a salesman quotes the retail price of a new car, there are, hidden behind that attractive facade of shining beauty, a veritable host of hidden taxes. The finished product is like a river that has been made up of hundreds of smaller streams and remote and tiny creeks. Who could even guess how many times, in the assembling of that car, for all its automatic gears, taxes have been manually shifted from the moment the first shovelful of ore was mined, or the first pound of sand was fired to make a lens for one of the lights? There were taxes on factories, machinery, tools, labor, sales and everything that was needed to put it all together. Any one with any imagination can see what the rescinding of all taxes on commodities would do in bringing down the high cost of living. In fact, the cost of living always goes up as the price of land advances.

The power of tax policy is double barreled. That ever present high cost of living bug-a-boo, involving high priced land and high commodity costs, is a result of our low land value tax and our high tax on labor products, for in addition to all those price increases, caused by the taxation of commodities, are all those added expenses caused by the high cost of land. In order to acquire land most people are obliged to borrow heavily because of the land cost. This involves a steady flow of interest over a period of many years, and much of their income is drained off to pay the mortgagee.

Nowhere in the United States is there anything like a tax on land value, exclusive of buildings. In Pennsylvania, the cities of Pittsburgh and Scranton have a tax policy, whereby city taxes (not School Board or County taxes) are so based that one half of the tax is based upon land value and the other half on the conventional method of using the combined value of both land and buildings together. This, therefore, was the chief reason that Pittsburgh was able to come up with that very unusual Golden Triangle development, long before billions of dollars were being made available by the Federal Government for urban renewal projects. Anyone who understands what a tax on land value could do is theoretically opposed to the nonsense of assuming that there ever will be enough tax-money in America to rebuild the parts of all our cities that suffer from obsolescence. This is one of the maddest concepts of our mad, mad world!

All of which brings us to a point where we ought to discuss a few fundamental aspects of taxation. Dr. Elizabeth E. Bowen has written a remarkable book which lives up to its title, *Economics Simplified.** There are a few paragraphs concerning the taxation of commodities upon which it would be difficult to improve:

"A tax is 'an enforced contribution levied on persons, property or income by the State, for government needs.' This sounds arbitrary and it is arbitrary. Any government can compel any citizen to give up any or all of his property for the support of the State. But here is a fund, made up of ground rents of the community, which rightfully belongs to all the members of the community; and to draw on this fund, which belongs to all, for the expenses of the government, the benefits of which are enjoyed by all, constitutes the only just tax possible.

"If we were not blinded by custom, what would we think of a community which ignored this fund, allowed it to be appropriated by anyone who could get it, and then, in order to support its government, appropriated the property of individuals without regard for equity or justice?

"Often the mistake is made of debating as to which of two given principles should be adopted in raising revenues in support of government—'Should taxes be levied in accordance with *ability to pay*, or, in accordance with *benefits conferred* on the tax-payer by the community?' This takes it for granted that there are only these two principles, but though few recognize it, there is in use today a third principle, and that is to tax in accordance with *need to buy*.

"Most of our direct taxes are levied, at least theoretically, in accordance with the citizen's supposed ability to pay. But most of our indirect taxes, which comprise the larger part of all taxes, are raised in accordance with this unrecognized third principle—necessity to buy. These taxes are passed along from one producer to another until they finally reach the ultimate consumer. He never knows how much he is paying in taxes, but he can be sure that the more he buys the more taxes he pays. A family which uses six loaves of bread a week will pay twice the amount of taxes included in the price of bread that will be

* Published by The Robert Schalkenbach Foundation—p. 166

paid by a family using but three loaves a week, though the latter family may be wealthy and the former very poor. Therefore, not even theoretically are these indirect taxes levied in accordance with ability to pay or in accordance with benefits conferred.

"Few realize how large a part of the price paid for a commodity consists of taxes levied on its production. For instance, in 1938, the prices of items named below included taxes as indicated (from computations of California Taxpayers' Association):

| In the price of | Number of taxes | In the price of | Number of taxes |
|---|---|---|---|
| Bread | 52 | Suit of clothes | 105 |
| Canned Fruit | 32 | Cotton dress | 125 |
| Sugar | 45 | Shoes | 126 |
| Beef | 127 | Overalls | 148 |
| Bar of soap | 154 | Wire fencing | 191 |
| Automobile | 145 | Milk of magnesia | 172 |
| Gas and oil | 205 | Some other drugs | 378 |

"If justice were its aim, no government should have any difficulty in deciding which of these principles to follow in raising its revenue. For to tax either in accordance with need to buy does not accord with justice. Both of these are based on the same motive which actuated the pirates to take, 'where the taking is good,' and that is the best that can be said for either of them. They penalize thrift and industry and injure everyone. The only payment any government can command, justly, from anyone, is payment for the advantages which the individual receives from the community in which he lives, i.e., payment for benefits conferred."

All these things being so, you can put this down as a fact of life: By taxing buildings and allowing the tax on land to remain low, we make both land and buildings expensive. By taxing land value and reducing the tax on buildings proportionately, we make both land and buildings cheaper. Thus, under a land-based tax, all individuals and firms will be able to build bigger and better buildings, and all will find more desirable land sites available at more reasonable prices.

We just stated one of the most zealously guarded secrets of modern times. We graduate tens of thousands every year from our colleges. If you were to ask any college graduate if a tax on land value would produce any effects, either different or better than a tax on buildings, you would probably be treated to a blank stare or a quizzical look that would seem to accuse you of asking a trick question. Most of them would say, "You must be kidding."

With the preceding concepts in mind let us re-emphasize a statement that was made in the previous chapter where we spoke of the differences between land and buildings, the true import of which may not have been realized. Land, being as it is, limited in supply, will sometimes increase thousands of percentage points in value. In many cities there are many square blocks easily worth one million dollars. There was a time when such land might have been bought for ten dollars. It may have taken one or two hundred years for this difference to develop, but whether it took one week or two hundred years is inconsequential. It should be borne in mind that each year, while the land was increasing in value, rents were being collected, becoming progressively greater with each passing year. There may have been some years of depression when the rents went down. Nevertheless, it is the same piece of land. The accrued value is the result of social and economic activity in that particular spot, as compared to some three-acre plot in some remote section in Western Kansas, fifty miles from the nearest town. Its worth is determined by its productive capacity. Not that it is capable of producing 500,000 bushels of wheat that might be sold at $2.00 per bushel, but because millions of people, living in the general vicinity, have enhanced its worth by their very presence and their willingness to go to that area in search of items in trade. This is the power of, this is the glory of land. In all parts of the so-called "free world" these socially created values are appropriated by landowners, as if they had rendered some Herculean service and were entitled to society's profound respect and adulation.

No such enhancement of value accrues to any manufactured item which can be reproduced at will. If more of the particular item in question is needed it will be produced on a "cost plus profit" basis. If the state were to take in taxes the full capital return on the production of any item, it would automatically wipe out any and all incentive for producing any more of the desired item. This is no way for the state to behave, especially in a democracy which is supposed to help and not hinder people in the process of producing wealth. However, if the state were to take even as much as 90% of the annual rental value of land in taxation, the result would be salutary rather than disastrous to the public at large. The land with its productive power would still be there. The demand for whatever the land might provide would still exist. The very need to live, a factor that landowners have exploited for centuries, would compel individuals to produce and encourage them to do so because they would be able to retain for themselves the entire product of their hands. If the state, by collecting 90% of the annual rental value of land, were enabled thereby to cease and desist from levying taxes against all manufactured items, the results could be seemingly miraculous but actually quite natural. This, of course, could not be possible until many revisions in our complicated relations between business and government might be made, but it certainly presents a fascinating prospect. The real beauty of such an arrangement would be that individual initiative and private enterprise would be gloriously retained and eventually we could get back to a position where we could praise, and not damn, the results of *laizzez-faire*.

Our failure to tax land value to the extent that we should is the chief reason that wealth has become concentrated in fewer and fewer hands. This, however, may not become transparently apparent until we have explained the law of rent. Few people in our modern world even know that such a law exists; many of those who do haven't the faintest idea how it works to disenfranchise citizens, both politically and economically, in every tradition-bound country in the so-called "free world."

CHAPTER FOUR

# The Law of Rent

We wish to talk now about the law of rent, one of the most significant processes with which human beings have to cope. Indeed, there can be no resolution of the problem of poverty unless the law is understood and intelligently dealt with. For a society to be ignorant of how the law works is to condemn many to abject poverty, while at the same time, a relatively few are enriched beyond imagination. Paradoxically, for a society to understand it and to deal with it intelligently with the general welfare in mind, it could become a boon to all. Not to understand its true function can be devastating. Wisely dealt with it can be the key to achieving as near a state of utopia as is possible for men who want freedom, independence, justice and free competition for all.

Failure on the part of society to deal with it intelligently has permitted the law to instigate more down right meanness and more ugly deviltry, and its operations, even though unknown and unrecognized, have been responsible for more acts of "cruel and unusual punishment," and more examples of "man's inhumanity to man" than any other law at work on the human scene. In the final analysis, we will never be able to deal effectively with the problems growing out of the gross inequities that plague us, unless, and until, we deal intelligently with the law of rent. This may sound like a "hyperbolic hyperbole" especially when so few people even know there is such a thing to begin with.

No one really has to understand the law or even know that one exists. It simply takes over and unless something is done about it in order to neutralize its iniquitous inequities all sorts of terrible things begin to happen. For all this, one cannot blame the law itself. There is that about it that is good. Indeed, because it is so inexorable it really contains the seeds of our social salvation. Only the failure of good men to understand it and to deal with it intelligently makes it appear to be the sinister force that it seems to be. All this may sound like a paradox, but as we proceed with our story we hope to make clear that without this law's operation we would never be able to fix reliably the price or worth of any land anywhere, for it is the law of rent that regulates the never ending competition for land. Those well-intentioned social reformers who try to correct the inequities of an economy without understanding the law of rent only tend to make things ultimately worse by destroying the delicate mechanism of the free market which is the basis of the free enterprise system. The modern trend toward calling upon governments to create agencies to minister to the needs of the poor, without paying any attention to the law itself, has all but destroyed any faith in the reliability of the free market to regulate effectively our economic affairs.

As an economic law its operations are inexorable. It has been at work for centuries in many countries, making a few people fabulously wealthy and many pitifully poor. Before two hundred years ago no one ever suspected there was a *law* which automatically channeled wealth into the hands of those who owned or controlled the land, although it was obvious that to own and control land was the key to wealth and power. It was less than one hundred years ago that a precise method of neutralizing the evil effects of this law was carefully presented in a book entitled *Progress and Poverty*. By this time you must know who he was! Yes, it was Henry George, our "world renowned philosopher-economist." But today, one hundred years after the publication of his great classic, most Americans do not know whether he was an American or an Englishman.

Those who understand how the law works know very well that, unless we deal with it intelligently, our highly vaunted civilization is doomed. We cannot long continue to ignore the law nor can we hope to solve our accumulation of social problems without coming to grips with it. In these days of ecological concern and of energy shortages we will have grave problems even after dealing with it properly. But deal with it we must! Individuals must be set free to look after themselves in the crisis times that loom ahead.

Having spoken about the law in these extravagant terms, we suspect that most readers will be saying to themselves, "What is he talking about anyway?" If my own private poll-taking is an accurate reflection of public understanding, I would guess that 99% of the people, educated or otherwise, could not give even an approximation to a formal statement of the law, nor could they even explain in the most general terms how it works. Upon being questioned, most thoughtful people will say that it is probably the law which indicates how much a landlord can charge for the use of a property. Such a vague answer is deplorably inadequate. How would you have answered that question?

## 2

For the most part, our explanation of the law will focus on the way it has functioned, first in England and then in America. We could have chosen any one of dozens of other countries but most Americans are familiar with English history. For this reason they will be able to relate easier to whatever conditions are mentioned.

Limited references to the law of rent will be found in all economics textbooks, but in our judgment the conventional economists have not given the law the attention it deserves. For many years it was thought that the law applied only to agricultural situations but today economists recognize that it is applicable to industrial and commercial areas as well. Why conventional economists have not realized the importance of dealing with the law is a puzzle to those of us who understand how significant it really is.

In 1776, a date remembered for something else by most Americans, a Scotsman, Adam Smith, published his famous book, *The Wealth of Nations.* His was the first serious attempt to trace the cause-and-effect relationships in economic life. After reading the book, James Mill, the father of John Stuart Mill, began to puzzle over Smith's apt observation that far too much of England's wealth "went to rent." That was Smith's way of saying that those who owned land were able to claim more than their rightful share of the wealth produced.

But it was David Ricardo, a student of James Mill, who really discovered the process, or, if you please, *the law* which accounted for the fact that far too much of the wealth, produced by labor on England's land, went to rent. His discovery represented an intellectual achievement which rated far more rave notices than it received. Were it not for those who were then, and are now, reluctant to have the news of his discovery broadcast, the name Ricardo might be better known than it is. Unfortunately, Ricardo himself was too much of a believer in the aristocratic way of life, and like many who have been confronted with the discovery since, he preferred not to have anything done about it.

## 3

To attempt a formal statement of the law without explaining how it works is usually an exercise in futility. Most people need some explanation. Here is a formal statement of the law: *The rent of any given piece of land is fixed by the excess of its productivity over the poorest land in use.* Does a reading of the statement send you into an ecstatic realization that at last the Sphinx has spoken? Probably not! So let us get on with the explanation and a few simplified illustrations.

There is, of course, a wide range of value difference between one farm and another, between one business site and another, and between one area where there are mineral or oil deposits and another where there are none. These differences in worth are usually measured by the dollars bid for the right to claim the values inherent in the land. This is all very elementary. What is not so elementary is the peculiar advantage which the ownership privilege confers upon the landowner, and the automatic disadvantage it imposes upon those who, not being owners, are hired to cultivate the land, or who elect to rent the sites, or who do the actual work of extracting the minerals or oil therefrom.

It was natural that Ricardo would investigate first the flow of rent in agriculture. It was in England with its huge castles and landed estates that the operation of the law was most easily observed. In Ricardo's time the industrial revolution had begun but its impact had not been too widely felt. Now, in each and any huge estate (there were many then with acres by the thousands and tens of thousands) there was certain to be both some very fertile land and some very unproductive land. There was always a thin, wavering, but real line called the margin of production, which separated the land profitable for use from the land that was too poor to be cultivated. Since according to the law of rent, "the rent of any piece of land is fixed by the excess of its productivity over the poorest land in use," a landowner could claim all the wealth over and above what could be produced on the least productive land in use. Therefore, his became the lion's share of production's value. It made no real difference whether he rented the land to another or chose to hire labor and supervise the work himself, he would collect "the excess" for himself. By whatever means he employed, in the end he could claim the excess which, in other words, represented "rent." This is what Adam Smith meant when he used the phrase, "most of England's wealth was going to rent."

How did this actually work out? Let us suppose that the landowner held some very fertile land upon which a given input of capital and labor could produce 100 units of wealth daily (an arbitrary figure), and also some less fertile acres yielding 60 units with the same application of capital and labor. Suppose further there were areas even less productive, some capable of producing 30 units and some perhaps as little as 10 units. Obviously, he could hardly afford to pay those working the low grade land as much as he might afford to pay those working the highest grade land. In such a case, no mere human being could figure out exactly who might be entitled to what. Only something as mysteriously wonderful as the open market could hope to compute such figures, because in actual experience such clearly recognizable lines of demarcation between the various grades of land could never be drawn. Land "grading" is anything but an exact science and, because of topographical and even geological differences, the same field could have two or more different grades of land.

Now let us see how these land discrepancies operated to give the landowner an almost inevitable, but unfair, advantage. Notice the predicament in which the workers found themselves as compared with the legally protected position of the landowner. The workers had nothing but their labor with which to bargain, and the pressure of iminent hunger was always upon them, whereas the landowner had the power to deny or grant permission to work on his land. He could grant permission to work on the "100 unit value" land or he could banish the worker to the"10 unit value" land. No matter! All he would have to pay either one would be ten units because that was all that was being produced on the least productive land in use. In other words, the pay given workers on the high value land would be the same as that being paid to workers on the marginal land.

A worker might have had a lot of physical muscle but he had no economic muscle at all. The landowner held all the power and furthermore it was guaranteed to him by law. All that was produced on all grades in excess of 10 units could be appropriated by the landowner as his rent, or his rightful (?) share as "owner." Now the formal statement of the law of rent becomes clearer. *The rent of any given piece of land is fixed by the excess of its productivity over the poorest land in use.*

Let us suppose a landowner has twenty workers. Five of them work on land that can produce 100 units of wealth within a given time, five on land that can produce 60 units, five on land that can produce 30 units and five on land that is capable of producing 10 units only. Inasmuch as any wealth in excess of that which can be produced on the least productive land in use may be claimed by its landowner as his "rent," each worker will get 10 units regardless of how much he actually produces. The landowner from the 100-unit land would pocket 90 units; from the 60-unit land, 50 units; from the 30-unit land, 20 units. As for the other five workers all that was produced on the 10 unit land would go to them since they were entitled to all that could be produced on the least productive land in use. However, to repeat a bit, all in excess of what could be produced on the least productive land will be claimed by the landowner as his "rent." His total rent-take on the entire estate would be 5 × 90 (450) plus 5 × 50 (250) plus 5 × 20 (100) which amounts to 800 units. Ten units of wealth apiece for each of the twenty workers against 800 units (80 to 1) for the landowner would hardly seem to meet the specifications for what is "right or fair." Nevertheless, this is what happens, and always has happened, where the unfair, man-made, no-tax policy on land value meets up with an economic law such as the law of rent. Inasmuch as this law comes into play and wreaks so much havoc in human affairs only where land is privately owned, it would hardly be accurate to call it a "natural" law. Actually, it is an artificially induced process which comes into play only wherever, and whenever, men agree among themselves to treat land as a commodity and to throw a canopy of protective law over the process to protect its chief beneficiaries.

If, upon reading this simplified illustration, you might begin to suspect that the implications are somewhat sinister, you are so right! However, we have been too kind! An English landowner in the 18th or 19th century who could boast of only twenty workers would hardly be worthy of the title "gentleman," for at that time landed estates often comprised from 10,000 to 100,000 acres. On such extensive holdings there would be many hundreds of people working for the landowner. This, however, would in no way change the wage of the individual laborer. None of the workers would be getting much more than might be produced on the least productive land in use. Much of the land might be held out of use by the wealthy landowner as a hunting preserve which would scarcely qualify it as being productive at all, and as such it represented no useful or social function.

If our illustration of how the law of rent brings to the landowner 800 units of wealth while the worker is getting 10, and if you raise the question as to whether even such a return would be enough to build and maintain those fabulous castles, enlarge our illustration to involve a 50,000 acre estate on which there were 500 workers instead of 20. Then the calculated "return" to the landowner would be 125 × 90 plus 125 × 50 plus 125 × 20 which would be 20,000 units worth of wealth for the landowner while the individual worker would still be getting only 10. No wonder the landowner lived in an ornate castle with servants to meet his every whim while most of the workers outside the castle lived in hovels!

## 4

All this will be dismissed by the conventionally-trained as a glorified over-simplification. If our illustration is really apt, why can't sensible people see it clearly and deal with it forthrightly? How could such ravages of monopolistic landownership go unchallenged? They did not—the reason being that the latent ambitions and drives of men of talent and ability urged not a few to break away from the castle complex and to strike out on their own. Why subject oneself to the whims of some overbearing landowner? Why not be one's own man? Although in those days, prior to the industrial revolution, before machines had taken over much of the back-breaking work, most of the people were land-bound, and although there were basically only two classes—the landowners and the landless workers—yet many opportunities were always presenting themselves to the more aggressive members of the castle-crews. They could break away to become weavers, tailors, or boot-makers. They could become fishermen, miners or miscellaneous craftsmen. Masons and carpenters were needed to build landowners' castles and buildings. Traders and merchants were needed to be conduits for silks or satins or exotic foods that were coming from all parts of the world, and that were being bought in unbelievable quantities by the landowning aristocracy.

However, the difficulties involved in breaking away from the castles were always horrendous at the outset, and the early days of independence were lean and sparse. The high rent claimed, since land was seldom sold, was the first road-block. The rent required would press the wage return of the entrepreneur down near the level of "ten units per," so that the effort to be free would hardly seem worthwhile. Still, one was independent and what could be sweeter than being "out from under?"

In the early days of the industrial revolution mechanical inventions began to take over the work of weavers and tailors, and factories began to spew out unheard of quantities of dry goods. The more able entrepreneurs soon discovered there was a silver lining to the rent clouds that had always plagued them before they became breakaways. Now that they themselves were employers, they were able to hire labor for the same wage as workers were getting in the castle complex. "Ten units per" was the established going wage rate. After all, that was all the workers could make by working for the landowners. Why, therefore, should the industrialists pay more? If the workers preferred not to work in a damp or stuffy factory, that was their problem! Let them go back to the land! However, many of the workers could no longer go back to the land. They had come to the factory in the first place because they had been excluded from the land and were unemployed. The wage rate that seemed like a silver lining to the factory owners was a message of despair to the individual workers. Nevertheless, it was this "happy circumstance" that enabled the factory owners to pile up fabulous profits and soon many were doing almost as well as the landowners, while the poor workers who produced the wealth shared little of it.

Had the procession of break-aways been visible to the naked eye, travelers would have seen numberless casualties along the way. However, some would win, and some would "make it big"—big enough to buy land from some of the improvident landowners who may have wasted their substance in high living, and so to become a landowner in what was then a landowner's paradise. This, indeed, represented the ultimate in dreams.

## 5

In our day modern economies have expanded far beyond what they once were and the importance of land is forgotten so that its significance in the economy is seldom mentioned. As one young college-trained man observed when I tried to draw his attention to the importance of land, "Land is no longer important in the economy. We are living in a time of high finance where production quotas and capital gains are the real things." Of course, I suspected he was still eating the fruits of the land, even though he was a salesman and far removed from the soil. He was either paying rent for his dwelling or a high price for land, and he was certainly paying taxes on his house and everything else which he needed. But his eyes had been closed by the complexities of the process and he failed to understand that the low tax on land is what is sparking all the taxes we all have to pay for the labor products that we buy.

During the 19th century the industrial revolution gathered momentum and a great change was gradually effected in the life-style of England. Even before that time, all tillable land had been gobbled up by a few and as the 18th century ended, the prestige and power of the "landed gentry" were well nigh absolute. Wages for the landless had been pressed down to what could be produced at the margin (the poorest land in use), and both farm workers and factory employees had to accept wages that had long since been determined by the law of rent. To be sure, not *all* workers had to be content with that basic subsistence wage, because some were more able than others and important responsibilities were delegated to them. This brought to some workers both higher wages and some personal prestige, especially in the eyes of their own peers. Parenthetically, we should add that all such wage increases more than pay for themselves and in no way lessen the rent-take of the owners. It was ever thus, even as it is today. The law of rent never entirely freezes the wages of the more gifted at the lowest possible level. It merely fixes the wages for Abraham Lincoln's "common people" who have no unusual attributes. The wages of others are graduated upward as the law of supply and demand might dictate. However, at best, all such wages and salaries are graduated up from the basic wage which is far too low to begin with.

With the low level that had been established by the law of rent, a new breed of acquisitive and power-hungry people began to surface in England. New mechanical techniques were being developed so that cotton and wool from across the Atlantic and as far away as Australia could be woven into cloth. The basic wage being as low as it was, the industrial sweat-shops in England sprang into existence and even children were cruelly exploited, being paid far less than subsistence wages. (In America we have done the same to women for years.) Those who could find no work on the land drifted into the cities. There, the conditions by modern standards, were well-nigh intolerable, but the urge to keep on living was strong, and the new class of industrialists and merchants was able to produce commodities cheaply and sell them at goodly profits to the more affluent people in England and other countries in Europe. It never occurred to the industrialists that they might create a lucrative market for themselves by granting higher wages to the workers who really deserved a share in the operation. Why should it? Such a thought never occurred to the landowners. Why should they be any different? Anyway, who had any idea why wages were so low to begin with? Besides, the poor are too tired and helpless to fight back and to increase the wages of the more able might result in their "catching on." No one, not even the rich, suspected that low wages had something to do with failure adequately to tax land values.

But the type of landlordism in England was destined to undergo a great change. As early as 1800 the settlement of vast areas of newly-discovered lands began to have its effect upon the economy of England. Even prior to the panic of 1873, this and other factors had begun to put the crunch on the economy, but it was during that year that the great agricultural depression actually began which lasted for twenty years. Because of new techniques in refrigeration, good beef came in great quantities from Argentina. Shiploads of wheat flowed in from Canada and the United States, forcing the price of home-grown wheat to half of its former price. Gradually, the intake of the great landed estates began to dwindle as capital and profits moved toward factories and mining and commercial activities, with their increased opportunities for profiteering on the labor of workers.

Many rural landowners shifted their financial operations to the cities without changing in the least their interest or desire to profit from owning land. They discovered that by owning land in a city their rent-take was greatly increased. Some rural landowners were so addicted to luxury that they continued to waste their substance and failed to make the necessary adjustments as the prices of agricultural products dropped. These watched their holdings gradually diminish while their smarter brethren put their money into city land and became enormously wealthy. The richest man in England today is The Duke of Westminster whose country estates are small compared to those of former days, but whose rental income from urban properties in Mayfair and Belgravia is fabulous. Nevertheless, the prestige that comes from owning agricultural lands is still strong and when wealth has been acquired in other ways many people still buy up agricultural lands and bask in the traditional glory that once prevailed, even though they are not the Midas-like sources of wealth they once were.

Today, great tracts of land in English cities are owned by prominent families who have stubbornly resisted many attempts to levy taxes on vacant and unused land. (If a property in England is not rented, no tax is required. One eight story building, brand new, has never been occupied by tenants and has never been taxed for eight years.) This policy has sent the price of England's land so high that no ordinary person can hope to buy sites for a home, and even public housing programs have come to a halt. At the same time this foolish policy has kept the wage scale so low that pressure by the Labor government for redress has brought on a wave of socialistic measures which, for the time being, may seem to have alleviated many of the grosser injustices but which, in the long run, only tend to knock things further askew. A fairly generous welfare system, a strong income tax, a system of medical care and a heavy inheritance tax have been instituted. Such ameliorative measures have eaten somewhat into the enormous wealth reservoirs of the "owning" class, but as long as the basic wage is kept at the margin of production level the plight of the workers continues to be precarious.

This is the ploy of the landowning class wherever such "palliatives" are demanded—to grant some here and some there, but to keep a firm grip on the land, come what may. To be completely fair to them we must admit that landowners in England often assumed a paternal interest in their tenants and in times of emergency lent a helping hand. It was a sort of private Medicare and it did indeed help the destitute over the rough spots. Socialistic measures act as substitutes for those non-contractual, paternal acts of private individuals, replacing them with legal and contractual acts of governmental agencies. Millions, both in England and America, would be loath to return to the caprice of personal charity.

It should be admitted at this point that insofar as some of this money has come to the government from income tax levies against rental income, such governmental hand-outs or subsidies may tend to put more money into circulation, but too often the money used is "born of the printing press" and so becomes inflationary. But the most insidious thing about the process is that as long as taxes are levied on labor products and not on land value, the end result is always the same—to increase the price of land and so to increase the rent-take of the owners of land. Therefore, as long as the cries for redress can be satisfied by granting mere subsidies, while all efforts to tax land values are resisted, the landowners can recoup much of the wealth that has seemingly been drained from their reservoirs. Those who understand these things know that purely socialistic policies in countries where private and monopolistic ownership of land is recognized as legal only tend to increase rents and land prices. Recently, the U.S. House of Representatives voted to kill the Office of Economic Opportunity, the once mammoth antipoverty agency which has disbursed 12½ billion dollars since its creation some ten years ago. Presumably, poverty was to be dealt a death blow, but there is more poverty in America today and land prices and rents are higher by far than they were then. We cannot regret that many were helped, but 12½ billion—down the drain of basic principle, without our having learned a thing—and caring less!

## 6

Harlan Trott, writing about Britain's problems in *The Analyst,** published by the Henry George School of Northern California, says, "Nowhere does the news from London pinpoint Britain's basic dilemma. Briton is suffering more than most civilized countries from the unequal rights of a small ruling class known sometimes as the Landed Gentry. Their racket is private monopoly in land. This makes Britain a nation of rent payers."

"What Britain is witnessing today is a replay of the class struggle that flared up in the twilight of the Edwardian era and is now being dramatized in public television's Masterpiece Theater production titled 'Upstairs-Downstairs.'

"Take the parliamentary election campaign of 1909, for example. The main issue was the Lords' veto of a national budget because it contained a small proposed token tax of a few pennies in the pound on all private land values.

* Vol. IX No. 2. May 1974

"Speaking in Limehouse before a roaring cockney crowd of dock workers, the Liberal Party's Chancellor of the Exchequer, David Lloyd George, attacked the House of Lords in these sobering words:

"It will be asked why 500 ordinary men—chosen accidentally from among the unemployed—should override the deliberate judgment of millions of people who are engaged in the industry that makes the wealth of the country. It will be asked who ordained that a few should have the land of Great Britain as a perquisite? Who made 10,000 people owners of the soil, and the rest of us trespassers in the land of our birth? Where did that table of the law come from? Whose finger inscribed it?

"The Upstairs class has successfully fought off every effort to tax its land values to support a national budget from that day to this. And Lloyd George's question still goes unanswered.

"You often hear people say: "Socialism got Britain into this fix. No. It's the other way around. Land Monopoly got Britain into Socialism.

"TV newscasts show hundreds of middle class British rent payers leaving their homeland, bag and baggage, going to the remote Commonwealth countries—going where they hope land is cheap.

"Could anything be more tragic—more illustrative of our economic unschooling—or our blindness to justice, than the fact that hundreds of British families whose industry has helped to make the wealth of the country cannot afford to live in their own land anymore?

"When will self professing Christian nations take to heart the prophesy of Isaiah: 'They shall not build and another inhabit. They shall not plant and another eat.' "

When we use the phrase "sociological conditioning" we refer to a psychological process that develops gradually, but which eventually becomes a state of mind which accepts the status quo and becomes something of a fixation in the public mind. Where land is privately held but *never taxed* the economic status of the landowner inevitably becomes very high and that of the landless very low. This conditioning process, however, is gradual, often taking hundreds of years to develop to its bitter fruition.

This is how it was in England after the coming of William the Conquerer and gradually the patterns of repression became fixed. Across the years there were periods of rebellion as kings and their baronial cohorts assumed too much power, but by and large, the wealth, power and influence of landownership persisted and grew. By the 18th century, entrenched cruelty had become a way of life, and sensitive souls must have cringed as great landed estates, with their huge castles and systematized exploitation of the landless, presented a most scandalous contrast between the affluence of the rich and the unbelievable degradation of the poor. It is difficult to understand how hard and unfeeling the so-called "nobility" could have been, and how the people were gradually induced to accept their lot so patiently. But it always seems to happen that way where land is privately owned. Once the power to hold and to control land is granted, rationalizations seem to appear and to justify the heavily disparate levels of being for the various classes in the establishment. As gradually the conditioning process sets in, those who control the land accept as a sort of divine right their power to enslave the landless, while their victims, in turn, grow docile. Unless outside influences impinge upon their lives (something which seldom happened in the remote countries prior to the 18th century) making the landless aware of more promising possibilities, they will "settle in" asking no questions and dreaming no dreams.

In the early years of servitude, dignity may have to be traded for security and the human spirit may suffer in the process, but after a time the might-have-been sense of personal worth begins to weaken and the state of inequality is accepted and embraced as a part of one's personal philosophy. If one is born into a family where the process of adjustment has been completed, the growing child feels no pain and suffers no sense of abuse. In those countries where no one can remember any other state than one of total exploitation, travelers from the outside world are appalled at the unquestioned acceptance of the most vicious forms of social degradation.

There was one notable exception. Coming out of the desert where the law of rent plays no part in life because land is not privately owned, and adopting the ways of those whom they had conquered, the Hebrew people were perplexed and baffled by the train of injustices that seemed to have gradually overwhelmed them,—they knew not why or how. But their prophets never ceased to cry out against the social evils of their day. They had been sociologically conditioned to a different way of life and for that reason became the only people in the history of the world who never ceased to "kick against the pricks." But that is another story that will have to wait for another book.

CHAPTER FIVE

# The Law of Rent in America

So much for our brief explanation of how the law of rent affected life in the British Isles. Conditions in America were, at the time of the Revolution, quite different. However, the law of rent was actively at work and was laying the ground work for massive trouble on the social scene. There is a world of difference between the social conditions that prevail in a new country where there is a seemingly endless supply of unused land, and conditions that prevail in a country whose institutions are old and in which wealth has become entrenched. The law had been at work in England for over a thousand years, and the wealth that had been produced by labor had been diverted into the hands of those whose claims rested upon *ownership of land* rather than upon *production of wealth.*

In America all was different. Vast areas of rich and fertile land awaited the hordes of Europe's dispossessed who would come in ever increasing numbers to acquire land, something which had been denied them in Europe. For hundreds of years great numbers of potentially able people had been condemned to poverty and servitude, and had learned from bitter experience that any amount of initiative and enterprise was useless in a landowners' paradise. Though few ever realized that the institution of landownership was the culprit that was "doing them in," they were fully aware that their plight was desperate indeed.

Europe had not been without its social idealists and despite the guillotine, the rack, the stake and the dank prisons, one idea had become fixed in the minds of most of the dispossessed. It was this: that before justice could prevail, men would have to gain the power to elect their own rulers, and thus bring about a division of political power. That, they thought, would do it. But that was before the days of Adam Smith, David Ricardo, John Stuart Mill or Henry George. No one then knew that there was such a thing as the law of rent, and that no true respite could be gained until there had been achieved a division of economic power as well as of political power. In fact, most educated people in the world are still ignorant of the machinations of the law, and so still imagine that if one political party fails to bring in a state of general well-being, another party will surely turn the trick.

It is little wonder that land-hungry Europeans became adept in acquiring and holding land. After all, they had all been schooled in the advantages involved in being a landowner. Some came to America with the idea of holding sway over hundreds of square miles of land, the ownership of which had been granted by the king himself. But it was not to be. Landownership, yes, but not on such a grand scale. One had to work hard to clear his land and make it worth owning and there were no unemployed who were so desperate that they would do such work for beggars' pay. Things were different, but the law of rent had not been rescinded.

In Old England, before the industrial revolution began to complicate the economic picture, the land had long since become the private preserve of a relatively few landowners, and opportunities for common labor to break away were limited. In the previous chapter we explained how a landowner was able to claim in rent all the wealth that was produced in excess of what could be produced on the least productive land in use, and why the basic wage of all workers, regardless of how much wealth they actually produced, was fixed at the margin of production. Without the use of a diagram we drew a word picture of the process, using hypothetical figures to distinguish the varying grades of land in use. In this over-simplified manner, we attempted to show how the unfair claims of the landowner could be demonstrated. But with the industrial revolution beginning to create economic waves hitherto unknown, and with the discovery of a vast continental expanse of unimproved land waiting to be settled, the operations of the law of rent cannot be adequately explained with such a simple illustration or formula. This is particularly true when we consider how the law of rent worked in America where the resistance to the industrial revolution was much more relaxed than in England.

In explaining how the law of rent had operated in England we were dealing with a country which had experienced no really dynamic changes for hundreds of years. By the time we took up the story land had already been concentrated in a few hands. Even though there were many laborers involved in various occupations, some working on 100-unit land and all of them working on land above the margin, we did not mention how increased numbers of laborers give to labor as a whole a superior power in producing wealth. However, as we approach the American scene we cannot overlook this fact because such a vast area of land was so quickly settled by so many individuals who were destined to become landowners, and because the industrial revolution was "in the wings" and about to impose its dynamic effects as the settlement of America progressed.

Perhaps we should employ the same type of progressive word-picture as we did in the previous chapter because we are writing for people who are well-educated about many things, even though woefully uninformed about the working of the law of rent. Some may feel that such an over-simplification might be a waste of time but there are aspects of the more complex economic picture that are more easily explained after the simple base lines have been laid down. At the same time there is a section of *Progress and Poverty* which is so graphic in its portrayal of the problems confronting the early settlers that we will work a few paragraphs into our story as we go along.

## 2

## A QUOTATION FROM HENRY GEORGE

"Here, let us imagine is an unbounded savannah, stretching off in unbroken sameness of grass and flower, tree and rill, till the traveler tires of the monotony. Along comes the wagon of the first immigrant. Where to settle he cannot tell—every acre seems as good as every other acre. As to wood, as to water, as to fertility, as to situation, there is absolutely no choice, and he is perplexed by the embarrassment of richness. Tired out with the search for one place that is better than another, he stops—somewhere, anywhere—and starts to make himself a home. The soil is virgin and rich, game is abundant,the streams flash with the finest trout. Nature is at her very best. He has what, were he in a populous district, would make him rich; but he is very poor. To say nothing of the mental craving which would lead him to welcome the sorriest stranger, he labors under all the material disadvantages of solitude. He can get no temporary assistance for any work that requires a greater union of strength than that afforded by his own family or by such help as he can permanently keep. Though he has cattle he cannot often have fresh meat, for to get a beefsteak he must kill a bullock. He must be his own blacksmith, wagonmaker, carpenter and cobbler—in short a "jack of all trades and master of none." He cannot have his children schooled; to do so he must himself pay and maintain a teacher. Such things as he cannot produce himself, he must buy in quantities and keep on hand, or else go without, for he cannot be constantly leaving his work and making a long journey to the verge of civilization; and when forced to do so, the getting of a vial of medicine or the replacement of a broken auger may cost him the labor of himself and horses for days. Under such circumstances, though nature is prolific, the man is poor. It is an easy matter for him to get enough to eat, but beyond that his labor will suffice to the simplest wants in the rudest way."

## A COMMENT

There is no way that such a stretch of land could be accurately graded but time and circumstances will eventually take care of that. For our purposes we will simply say that in due time the differences will become more clearly defined and, for the moment, we will arbitrarily put a value on land in the entire area. Let us say that some land, with the same application of labor, time and capital, will produce 100 units of wealth; some will produce 75 units, some 50 and some 25. Our first settler quite logically elects to settle on 100-unit land.

## A FURTHER QUOTATION FROM GEORGE

"Soon there comes another immigrant. Although every quarter section of the boundless plain is as good as every other quarter section, he is not beset by any embarrasssment as to where to settle. Though the land is the same, there is one place that is clearly better for him than any other place, and that is where there is already a settler and he may have a neighbor. He settles by the side of the first comer, whose condition is at once greatly improved, and to whom many things are now possible that were before impossible, for two men may help each other to do things that one man could never do.

"Another immigrant comes and, guided by the same attraction, settles where there are already two. Another, and another, until around our first settler there are a score of neighbors. Labor has now an effectiveness which in the solitary state it could not approach. If heavy work is to be done, the settlers have a log rolling, and together accomplish in a day what singly would require years. When one kills a bullock the others take part of it, returning when they kill, and thus they take fresh meat all the time. Together they hire a schoolmaster, and the children of each are taught for a fractional part of what similar teaching would have cost the first settler. It becomes a comparatively easy matter to send to the nearest town, for someone is always going. But there is less need for such journeys. A blacksmith and a wheelwright soon set up shop and our settler can have his tools repaired for a small part of the labor they formerly cost him. A store is opened, and he can get what he wants as he wants it; a post-office, soon added, gives him regular communication with the rest of the world. Then comes a cobbler, a carpenter, a harness-maker, a doctor; and a little church soon arises. Satisfactions become possible that in a solitary state were impossible. There are gratifications for the social and the intellectual nature—for that part of the man that rises above the animal. The power of sympathy, the sense of companionship, the emulation of comparison and contrast, open a wider, and fuller, and more varied life.

"Go to our settler now, and say to him: 'You have so many fruit trees which you planted; so much fencing, such a well, a barn, a house—in short, you have by your labor added so much value to this farm. Your land itself is not quite so good. You have been cropping it, and by and by it will need manure. I will give you the full value of all your improvements if you will give it to me and go again with your family beyond the verge of settlement.' He would laugh at you. His land yields no more wheat or potatoes than before, but it does yield far more of all the necessaries and comforts of life. His labor upon it will bring no heavier crops, but it will bring far more of all the other things for which men work. The presence of other settlers—the increase of population— has added to the productiveness, in these things, of labor bestowed upon it, and this added productiveness gives it a superiority over land of equal natural quality where as yet there are no settlers."

## A COMMENT

For the moment Henry George is not concerning himself with what might be happening to settlers who have come too late to appropriate 100-unit land. When all the 100-unit land is taken up the late-comers face a "revoltin' development." They discover that 100-unit land is no longer free and if they wish to settle on free land they will have to go to the 75-unit land. Then, although they might work as hard as those on the 100-unit land they will be able to produce only 75 units of wealth. Under such conditions the first settler, upon being offered such a deal as referred to heretofore, would have added reason to laugh. Now his land will have a rental value and should he wish to sell to the buyer he would demand a price for the land in addition to the price offered for all his improvements. Moreover, that price would include an expectation or speculative factor and a buyer would be required to pay an additional amount for the mere prospect of enjoying the privileges and emoluments of ownership.

In these early stages of settlement, as lands of less and less productiveness are brought into use, all areas except the least productive ones in use will have developed rental values. Very simply, it works like this. Until all 100-unit land is taken up, wages will be 100 for all workers and rent will be zero. When new immigrants are obliged to settle on 75-unit land the wages in the entire area will be 75 units and rent will be 25 on the 100-unit lands. When newcomers are obliged to settle on 50-unit land the rent on 100-unit land will be 50, and that on the 75-unit land will be 25. Wages on all lands will have gone down to 50 units which means that those on 50-unit land can keep all they produce (their wages). When eventually 25-unit land is brought into production the wages on all lands will be 25 units, whereas rents on the 100-unit land will be 75, on the 75-unit land will be 50, and on the 50-unit land will be 25. Granted that this is an over-simplification it does indicate a basic trend and a general truth. However, it is not the whole truth because it fails to consider how, when population increases and there develops a higher degree of collaboration of all concerned in the production process, labor develops a greater power in production. This is highly significant as George goes on to explain.

## A FINAL QUOTATION FROM GEORGE

"Population still continues to increase, and as it increases so do the economies which its increase permits and which in effect add to the productiveness of the land. Our first settler's land being the center of population, the store, the blacksmith's forge, the wheelwright's shop, are set up on it, or on its margin, where soon arises a village, which rapidly grows into a town, the center of exchanges for the people of the whole district. With no greater agricultural productiveness than it had at first, this land now begins to develop a productiveness of a higher kind. To labor expended in raising corn, or wheat, or potatoes, it will yield no more of those things than at first. But to labor expended in the subdivided branches of production which consists in distribution, it will yield much larger returns. The wheatgrower may go further on and find land on which his labor will produce as much wheat, and nearly as much wealth. But the artisan, the manufacturer, the storekeeper, the professional man, find that their labor expended here, at the center of exchanges, will yield them much more than if expended even at a little distance away from it; and this excess of productiveness for such purposes the landowner can claim, just as he could in its excess of wheat-producing power. And so he is able to sell as building lots some of his acres for prices which they would not bring for wheatgrowing if the land's fertility had been multiplied many times. With the proceeds he builds himself a fine house and furnishes it handsomely. That is to say, to reduce the transaction to its lowest terms, the people who wish to use the land build and furnish the house for him, on condition that he will let them avail themselves of the superior productiveness which the increase of population has given to the land.

"Population still keeps on increasing, giving greater and greater utility to the land, and more and more wealth to its owner. The town has grown into a city—a St. Louis, a Chicago or a San Francisco—and still it grows—production is here carried on upon a great scale, with the best machinery and the most favorable facilities; the division of labor becomes extremely minute, wonderfully multiplying efficiency; exchanges are of such volume and rapidity that they are made with the minimum of friction and loss. Here is the heart, the brain of the vast social organism that has grown up from the germ of the first settlement. Here, if you have anything to sell, is the market; here, if you have anything to buy, is the largest and choicest stock . . . here, in short, is a center of human life, in all its varied manifestations."

"All those advantages attach to the land;" (or, as we would put it, *increase the value* of land) "it is on this land and no other that they can be utilized, for here is the center of population—the focus of exchanges, the market place and workshops of the highest forms of industry. The productive powers which density of population has attached to this land are equivalent to the multiplication of its original fertility by the hundredfold and the thousandfold. And rent, which measures the difference between this added productiveness and that of the least productive land in use has increased accordingly. . . .

"To recapitulate: The effect of increasing population upon the distribution of wealth is to increase and consequently to diminish the proportion of the produce that goes to labor in two ways: First, by lowering the margin of production. Second, by bringing out in land special capabilities otherwise latent and by attaching special capabilities to particular lands.

"I am disposed to think that the latter mode, to which little attention has been given by political economists, is really the more important."

END OF QUOTATION FROM GEORGE

If it were not for the way the law of rent tends to fix the basic wage of labor at the margin and to bring about a graduated increase of rents according to the productive capacity of particular lands, the economic conditions which develop as the population increases would be quite different. There is no truth in the contention that the increase of population, in and of itself, tends gradually to diminish the supply of wealth that can ultimately be divided amongst producers. Ten men, because of the division of labor, can produce more than ten times as much as one man, and by the same token, one thousand men can produce more than one thousand times as much as one man.

3

Why is it that, when currently acknowledged experts meet to discuss such matters as world hunger, they invariably assume that population pressure is the main issue? Our answer to this is that they have no comprehension as to how the law of rent works. Where there is a minimum of complexity and very little industrial development, as was the case in Old England, wages are always at a minimum because the pressure of population has lowered the margin of production by bringing very poor land into use. In such cases wages remain at a bare subsistence level, not only on poor land but on the highest grades as well. However, in the United States, as population increased and the division of labor was perfected to the nth degree, and as vast improvements in the arts of production were effected, all of which was accompanied with fantastic advances in education and cultural achievements, the power of labor to increase wealth was little short of fantastic. This is reflected in a higher basic wage to labor at the margin, so that the average man with no unusual talents or abilities can, if he is working at all, enjoy a much higher standard of living than his counterpart of three hundred years ago. Although wages are still determined by the productivity of labor at the margin, it is possible for labor to produce more wealth at the margin than it might have done had none of the things that denote progress ever occurred. Moreover, in our stage of civilization, labor has the power to increase wealth on all grades of land, so that the rent-take is many times greater than it was when times were simple and uncomplicated. Lands originally graded at 100, 75, 50, and 25 would, now that labor can produce 100 times as much wealth as before, produce 100 times as much on all grades. The basic wage would then have been increased to 2500 (25 × 100) and the rent-take on 50-unit land would be 2500 (25 × 100, as much as labor), on 75-unit land it would be 5,000 (50 × 100, twice as much as labor), and on 100-unit land it would be 7,500 (75 × 100, or three times as much as labor). Let anyone who is inclined to brush impatiently aside such figures as being inapplicable in our modern economy consider that the landowner or landowners (most of them do no work anyway) of the site of the Socony-Mobil building in New York may be taking in rent $500,000 annually. One does not have to have a certified list of the earnings of those who work in that building to know that the average wage of all those employed is nowhere near that figure. A few might be receiving from $200,000 to $500,000 but most of the workers would be receiving less than $30,000 and the great majority, less than $10,000. Strange as it may seem to many who do not understand the law of rent, the theory will always be justified by the facts.

Our purpose in using the arbitrary land grading figures was to bring this point out as simply and clearly as possible. Quite naturally, labor gets more of this world's goods than before, but although it does receive a greater quantity in wages it is not recompensed as it should be. Rent still claims its disproportionate share and the amounts are staggering. The average man has a very limited appreciation of how much of the wealth of the country goes to rent.

## 4

To any discerning reader, the advantage of being the first to arrive is apparent. It is by virtue of their position as owners, and not as producers of wealth, that those who made the scene early are in a position to levy a daily toll upon the labors of those who were late in arriving. This is a constant and continuous process and with every day's work from that moment on, the first to arrive will take in rent a portion of that which those who work on their land produce. To make things worse and to compound the unfairness of such a process, the rent factor will keep going up and the wage factor will keep going down as a proportion.

In every new community there were those who, having arrived early, enjoyed the steady stream of wealth which came to them in rent. To their taking of this portion of the wealth that was being produced there was no opprobrium attached. It was their right! No one really understood why the wage level in any community was what it was. They only knew it was as it was. No one ever questioned the right of any landowner to take what, in the system of things, was his to demand. So, the Mr. Earlys and the not-quite-too-lates proceeded to appropriate what society agreed was their proper right. Now that we understand we may conclude that it was hardly fair, but that was how it was done. In due time, as those who owned land claimed their daily toll in rent, the money-flow began to move in the direction of those who owned land and the cumulative process was greatly accentuated as land values, especially in the cities, began to rise.

With such vast areas of land being settled, and that mostly in hunks of from one hundred to three hundred acres, and with this division of land being made among hundreds of thousands of people over millions of square miles of territory, it is little wonder that, for a while at least, most of the traditional bonds which had ruined life in other parts of the world were shattered. America became the miracle of the ages. "Freedom" became the watchword which seemed to characterize its mood. But it was not, as many would have us believe, due entirely to free enterprise, although that certainly was a factor. We should never forget that it was the abundance of free land that made it all possible.

With landownership being thus so widely distributed, it would have taken many more decades than it actually did for the ubiquitous and gravity-like pressure of the relentless law of rent to bring about a dangerous concentration of wealth and power. But the business world was on the verge of exploiting a whole new world of technical discoveries. All sorts of industries were being formed, resulting in an unbelievable explosion of human energy. Never in history had there been such head-over-heel activity. It was a period of widespread experimentation and while many entrepreneurs made mistakes that proved very costly, the overall momentum for the economy in general was nothing short of sensational. This process accelerated the growth of great cities in which land values zoomed to fabulous heights. Besides, raw materials were needed to supply the factories and this put a sometimes fabulous value premium on other land areas that had previously been devoid of much value.

With our inexorable law of rent working behind the scenes, common labor could be hired by manufacturers for wages commensurate with those being paid to farm hands. (The gross amount paid would be higher, but the net return, after paying rent and buying food, would be about the same.) Thus, industrialists in America as in England discovered that wages need not be calculated on actual production worth but only upon what anyone might produce on the best free land in use. This enabled manufacturers to make sizable profits which, in the final analysis, came from their unquestioned and legal right to withhold wages that might have been based upon production worth. Industrial growth advanced rapidly, resulting in the movement of population into urban centers and accelerating the tempo toward inequity. Without this new industrial activity it might have taken centuries before wealth and power had become as dangerously concentrated as it had become in England, whereas, under these new circumstances, it took only a matter of decades.

Although in many cities growth was slow and steady, in some it was very rapid. Perhaps San Francisco provides the most spectacular example of a city that grew rapidly, with Chicago running a close second. However, in San Francisco the growth was so swift and the workings of the law of rent were so clearly demonstrated that we would do well to review what happened.

In 1848 there were 800 inhabitants. Two years later the population was 16,500. Arthur Nicholas Young, in his book, *A History of the Single Tax in the United States,* quotes an interesting passage culled from *The Annals of San Francisco:* "After recounting the big gains which men got in gold mining, merchandising and loaning capital at thirty or sixty percent, we find that it was the holders of real estate who made the greatest fortunes. The possession of a small piece of ground in or about the center of the city was a fortune in itself. Those lucky people who held lots from the time before the discovery of gold, or who shortly afterwards managed to secure them, were suddenly enriched, beyond their first sanguine hopes. The enormous rents paid for the use of ground and temporary buildings in 1849 made all men covetous of real estate. . . .

"The temptation to perpetuate any trick, crime or violence, to acquire real estate seemed to be irresistible, when great returns drawn from it were considered. . . . The rents of the larger hotels, coffee saloons, gambling houses and billiard rooms, and of the finer stores, offices and dwelling houses were rented at equally extravagant sums. . . . In a couple of years, the building speculator in real estate had all his outlay (which, since labor and materials were so very high, was exceedingly great) returned to him in the shape of rents. Henceforward his property was a very mine of wealth. As rents rose, so did the price of such property. The richest men of San Francisco have made the best portion of their wealth by the possession of real estate."

Thus it would appear that a relatively few men, either because they had enough money to gain entrance to the mythical landowners' club, or because they had arrived on the scene early enough to have acquired sites that suddenly became very valuable, were in a position to begin collecting "the excess" of what any tradesman or merchant could produce on the least valuable land-site in use. This collection process was not just a "one shot deal." It was to be repeated, month after month, and was to become a constant and continuous money-flow from those who did all the work to those who merely held a title-deed to the land.

When population increased and the tempo of business activity was stepped up in any vicinity, the amount of rent-take was based upon the earning power of the land and not on the productive power of the working force. Just to make certain that this would be the case, in many leases an escalator clause would be included. As sales increased the rent would go up. Thus, the owner would make sure that he would get all of "the excess" to which, by law, he was entitled. He may have developed no expertise in the business or trade of the tenant, but his ownership of the land put him in a position to "cut himself in" on all the earnings "in excess" of what the various employees might be able to produce on the least productive landsites in use.

All this is reminiscent of the favorable position of the 100-unit farmer after all the land except the 25-unit land had been taken. He could demand 75 of the 100 production units and call it rent. But the earning power of farm land is downright skimpy compared to that of a five million dollar site in a huge city. We are now in the big league! That top 100-unit land is peanuts and the rent-take is chicken feed compared to the return from the city site. An acre of good farm land might cost $400 but an acre of choice city land could cost anywhere from $50,000 to $5,000,000. Hundreds of people could be working on the city land and the rent-take would be a fortune because, in the final analysis, wages are computed on that basic wage that has been determined by the law of rent at the margin. By no means does everyone receive only that "basic wage." Some will be paid for any special ability or skill which they may have to offer. After all, the owner will be willing to pay more to a store manager than to a floor sweeper (the average man with no talent or unusual ability). He can afford to do so because a skilled worker will actually produce much more wealth, so that the owner is repaid in the added amount of wealth produced. In this world labor is worthy of *more* than its current hire.

A huge office building will house many kinds of tenants, The landowner may know very little about the law but he will cut himself in on the earnings of all the lawyers in the building. He may know only as much about medicine as he has gleaned from aspirin or cough-repressant advertisements, but he has the ever-operating law of rent on his side. Therefore, he can cut himself in on the earnings of the physician and his entire staff. We can curl our lips in scorn as we mention the nefarious activities of gangsters and racketeers, but at the central point of our economic system there is a "racket phase" of life that must, in due time, bring society to its knees. As long as we accept the institution of private ownership of land as valid we must accept the fact that rent must be paid for land use. Rent is what it is regardless of who it is that gets it. When a private citizen alone is the rent-taker the rent will be just as high as it would be if the government were levying a tax on land value and so claiming a larger share of the rent. The point is that when we pay as much as 90% of the rent to the state instead of 100% to the landowner, the state can then reduce the taxes which we otherwise might be obliged to pay on the buildings and improvements. The landowner would have enough to repay himself for his management and judgment, but he would not be in a position to claim for himself the values created by the workers involved in the use of the land. Why should anyone have to pay tribute to any individual merely because he or his grandparents got there first?

## 5

Any discerning reader should be able to see the enormity of this widespread rent-take process when he realizes how many towns and cities have come into existence within the past one hundred years. We have talked about the central city sites where values have zoomed, but there are millions of sites of lesser value which are still far more valuable than most farm land. As long as assessors fail to assess land at its true value, and as long as taxing authorities follow the unscientific policy of collecting taxes on *improvements,* the law of rent does it's worst. Those who benefit the most are the big corporations with their vast stretches of timber, oil and coal lands and owners of very valuable city sites and vacant urban land. They are the royal families of our modern economy. Owners of homes may think that they benefit by our inverted tax policy but they are heavy losers. They paid far too much for their sites to begin with and because homeowners put their hearts and souls into their homes they are obliged to pay excessive taxes on all their improvements. Meanwhile, owners of unused and vacant land strangle the economy and deny millions of people the joy of having well appointed homes for comfortable living. A full and complete tax on land value and a near total remission of taxes on buildings and commodities would go far toward affecting such changes as are necessary. The process is so simple that it is a crying shame that ill-informed incumbents in state and federal legislatures keep stumbling along, passing innumerable laws, and setting up overlapping bureaus in an effort to correct abuses here, and just plain malfunctions there. Unfortunately, those who benefit constantly exert their enormous influence toward hushing up those who insist upon pointing up the damage that is being done to ninety-five percent of the population by the gross favoritism being shown nonproducing landowners.

Now that pioneer days are over, there are millions of citizens in this country who arrived too late. Millions of us are paying through the nose to the second and third generation descendants of the original owners of key landsites. Many of them produce nothing! Every city has its quota of absentee landowners. They live high on the withheld wages of those who toil on what the law says is *their* land. But the law is in error, The land should ideally be recognized as the gift of the Creator to all men. We should think of it as "our land." Unless we get around to acting intelligently on the realization of this fact, we have no chance at all of working our way out of the morass into which we have fallen. This is not socialism. And it is a million miles away from communism. But it is the only way we can hope to retain the free enterprise system which most people regard as the keystone of capitalism.

We have not yet even tried to show how a scientifically instituted tax on land value, along with a total remission of taxes on buildings and improvements,would effectively serve to correct our current condition. These matters will be our concern in the next few chapters.

If, after all that has happened in the past few years, any individual does not realize that we must deal effectively with gross inequity, there is little that we can say or do to influence his thinking. Unless we succeed in redistributing the wealth, not only in America but throughout the world, the present age of man is doomed. In pointing up the processes that cause this gross inequity and in recommending practical ways of dealing with them, we not only redistribute the wealth but guarantee that we will no longer allow most of the wealth to go to the rent-takers.

Upon the arrival of The Great Depression, which marked the end of an era, the strains in the economy were so great that new and tradition-breaking policies were instituted. "They may alleviate conditions for a time but they will have no lasting or corrective effects" was the often repeated comment of my own mentor as he coached me in the basic principles of Georgist philosophy. He was right. It was merely a holding action and little real reform was involved. Although the desperate straits of the very poor and unemployed were somewhat relieved, the economy limped along for over a decade. Then came the second world war and the traditional method of raising money for armament and to pay for military action was employed. The national debt rose by leaps and bounds. Even though the sinews of war were dug out of the ground and put together by the work and sweat of millions during those hectic years, the bill was met by bond issues which sent the national debt soaring. The enormous expenditures of the government in meeting the exigencies of the times had already pushed the debt up to unheard-of heights, but there had never been any other way to defer payments for the unexpected and the extraordinary.

A few significant things occurred to stimulate economic activity. Labor unions were granted many legal rights hitherto withheld. Wages in the major sectors of the economy were increased over most of the years since the depression. This did create a market for goods and greatly stimulated production. These increases were not specifically related to actual production figures but there is little doubt that but for the higher wage levels resulting from labor organization the growth of the economy would have been greatly restricted.

New inventions came along to create an enormous expansion of industry. The radio, the new techniques in the reproduction of sound, and finally the television industry put millions to work, and these, along with the rise in the use of automobiles, the building of roads and the establishing of sales and service agencies, did create great economic activity. Had it not been for the new inventions and the perfecting of highly desirable products which everybody longed to possess, the coming of the depression might have forced us to go to the basics long since. But human beings are loath to institute basic and unconventional correctives unless there seem to be no other alternatives.

It is possible that some inventions might come along to activate the economy and keep it afloat for another period. Since the publication of the first printing of this book the computers, both large and small, have been taking the country by storm. Many millions of small computers have been sold and the enormous potential for economic stimulus is suggested in an article in TIME,* "It is estimated that there are at least 25,000 applications of the computer awaiting discovery. Notes *The Economist:* to ask what the applications are is like asking what are the applications of electricity.'"

* Time, February 20, 1978. P. 49 of Time

CHAPTER SIX

# The Law of Rent Around the World

George R. Geiger, in his book *The Philosophy of Henry George*,* says that George accepted the Ricardian law of rent as possessing "the self evident character of a geometric axiom, and found that the ownership of land, unlike the ownership of capital, conveys the ability to appropriate part of the product without the expenditure of productive effort, for rent is simply the result of the bidding on the part of both labor and capital for a fixed land supply." George himself insisted that the principle was so clear that "there is no necessity for discussion." "Of course," says Geiger, "Modern economics has found quite some necessity for discussion." He says that George's "interpretation of rent was completely the classic one and, being based upon his clear separation of land from capital, was considered as the return solely to land."

In the opening section of his great classic, *Progress and Poverty*, George carefully defined all basic terms and agreed to use them precisely as defined. Any imprecise failure to distinguish clearly between land, labor products (wealth) and capital (stored up labor being used to produce more wealth) could lead to confusion. Unfortunately, much of the confusion that seems to prevail in economic understanding is due to a widespread failue to accurately define basic factors involved in the economic process. If land is wealth and if there is no difference between land and labor products, as most texts imply, there is little we can do to clarify or enlighten. If any author discounts as inconsequential the law of rent and tries to reason his way through what cannot be other than a "jargon jungle" his state must ultimately become one of "confusion worse confounded."

Once a person grasps the truth of Ricardo's law of rent he understands precisely why some nations are bogged down in the mire of gross inequity, with only a few owning and controlling both land and wealth, while the masses are impoverished and illiterate. Indeed, unless the student accepts this law as a "geometric axiom" he cannot account for the same tendencies manifest in our own sophisticated economy."

In many countries across the world in which landowners have traditionally owned and controlled both land and wealth, and where they are themselves in complete control of the government, the masses are virtually helpless. Where

* Footnote on p. 111.

the democratic process has never joined battle to ease the burdens of the people, and where ameliorative reforms have never been instituted, the harsh outlines of the law of rent are clearly visible to those who understand the law. The pity of it is that those writers and reporters, whose duty it is to explain what is going on in those countries, are usually oblivious to the basic causes of the most significant world events. We suspect that most writers have never even heard of the law of rent, or if they have, have never understood how unrelenting its processes actually are. They seldom mention, nor do they attach any significance to the fact that the landowners literally control the government. Consequently, most writers fail to put things in proper perspective.

This myopic condition characterizes not only the editorial writers and commentators on radio and television but most of the influential members of the so-called establishment. One would get the impression that no one in any high place in government, in education, in religion or in the public media had ever heard of Henry George or that there is any difference at all between the nature of land and that of labor products. The official attitude of the government seems to be one of uneasy tolerance for those aspects of repression that are exercised by officials in those countries where the law of rent has gone unchecked for centuries. The essential consideration seems to be that as long as a country is committed to a policy of private ownership of land, this and this alone, qualifies a country to enjoy nominal membership in the "Free World Club." The reason is obvious enough. It is not that our own citizens are necessarily owners of land in other countries and so would suffer the slings and arrows of confiscation, but rather that any and all deals that might be made with a country that no longer recognizes the rights of citizens to own land would be impossible and meaningless. Without a policy of entente the doors to any natural resources involved will be slammed shut. This explains why our country makes deals that seem to justify outrageously unjust conditions. We could at least refuse to make loans or give aid to regimes that are so obviously repressive. But who is to determine the reason for the repression? Moreover, even if we really knew what the cause of the trouble was, who could expect us to say anything about the need for some other country to undertake the proper kind of land reform when we refuse to do anything about it ourselves? The trouble would seem to be that so few people understand that there is such a thing as the law of rent, and failure to deal with it intelligently has diminished all hope of freedom, of justice and of social well-being, not only in the underdeveloped countries but in our own country as well.

Here again we are confronted by the fact that the great majority of educated people in this country know nothing about the law of rent. They cannot define it; they cannot explain how it works nor can they recognize the symptoms of its operations. If wealth in any country has clotted and the great majority of the people are living below the poverty line, the explanations of those being queried are as diverse as their knowledge is scant. Ask any of your college trained friends why the backward countries are as they are. They will fumble around and offer you symptoms for reasons. Some will blame it on bad governments—as if the landowners were so busy with their crops that they couldn't care a hoot what the government was doing—some will blame it on bad religion, some on over-population, some on lack of proper tools and others on lack of proper educational facilities. The fact that there is a mistakenly held belief that landowners should take full advantage of an uncontrolled law of rent and use it to exploit and tyrannize their fellowmen will never be mentioned.

## 2

In Latin and South America the early settlers were adventurers in search of gold. They were mostly Spanish and Portuguese. Never having been through the fires of a full fledged reformation, they were not concerned about bettering their social and religious lives as were many immigrants who came to North America. Many came with official land grants from their kings and managed to make them stick, something which the settlers in North America were unable to do because land hungry Europeans refused to honor such grants. They kept fanning out in all directions, claiming squatter's rights and establishing those rights by clearing and cultivating the land.

Today, after three hundred years, the law of rent has done its work in South America. A few landowners own all the land that is worth owning. The people have been disinherited and live in the poverty or sub-poverty zones. Wages are minimal and only the rich and their henchmen can afford to buy an American car, due to incredibly high tariffs. Not knowing of any other presumed correctives except state socialism or out-and-out communism, the would-be reformers have given it their best shot, only to be defeated and demoralized at every turn. All over Latin and South America the landowners have set up fascist dictatorships and are practicing such violations of human rights as the so-far relatively safe North Americans wouldn't believe. But, although the process has not *yet* run full circle in our country, our time is coming. It may take several years before that evil day dawns for us, but some unforeseen crisis such as a full-blown depression or another world-threatening war might well compact those several years into several days or weeks. There are powerful elements across the world who would eagerly give impetus to the blotting out of our freedoms, just as there are many in our own country whose patriotism has been tarnished by greed who are glad to take advantage of the people in South America when the local leadership tightens the screws. Now they can, with our taxes and the C.I.A., safely invest their millions.

So it goes today in South America. Do the educated people of this country have a clear picture of it all? Do they even understand what happened in Russia before the communist takeover? They will get close enough to suggest that since all the land was owned by the aristocrats the peasants finally rebelled. They will say that the government had become corrupt; the rich were heartless, the masses were destitute and the church was ever on the side of the aristocracy. Seldom will anyone suggest that landowners, operating under an uncontrolled law of rent, had so effectively deepened the plight of the peasant class, and at the same time so completely preempted all the arable and useful land, that all hope of future well-being was destroyed among the masses. They will never mention the law of rent. How could they? Their teachers never told them there was such a thing in the first place. WHY? Certainly not because they knew and preferred to keep the ugly truth to themselves.

They never knew that taxes on land value could not be passed on; that taxes on commodities were always passed on; that, in consequence, the more land is taxed, the cheaper it becomes, while the more commodities are taxed, the more expensive everything we buy is certain to be. As the business cycle spirals upward they watch the price of land steadily increasing until toward the end, when people begin talking about a possible depression, they realize that the inflation of land values was making it all but impossible to buy sites for homes or stores. Strange, isn't it, that the establishment press or leadership never seem to equate this fact with the condition known as inflation?

Tens of thousands of American tourists go to foreign countries and have opportunities to observe how people in other countries live. How many Americans ever think of equating social conditions which vary from country to country with the operations of the law of rent? If social conditions are deplorable how many ever check to see whether or not there is any tax on land value? Where there is no tax at all on land value one can be certain that practically all taxes are based upon labor products or, as economists would say, "on production." If a relatively small segment of the population owns the land; if the price of land is shockingly high and if the majority of the people are living in abject poverty, one can be certain, without even asking, that land is not taxed and landowners are, as Louis XIV would say, "the state." In other words they make the laws and literally run the country.

When someone told me that in El Salvador, a Latin American country of about two million inhabitants, following the coffee harvest only six families pick up all the checks, I knew there was a no-tax policy on land value. It could not be otherwise! Upon viewing a motion-picture travelogue on Spain and Portugal I knew that in those countries there was a no-tax policy on land value. You may be sure that the Maharajas of India could never have monopolized the land if there had been any tax on land value. India presents one of the most graphic showcases of what happens where, over a long period of time, landowners enjoy land value tax immunity under the law. Splendor for a few and squalor for the many are the fruits of such a policy!

3

Today the plight of millions around the world is desperate. The governments, even in North America—the citadel of freedom—are less and less able to protect their citizens. Crimes of violence are erupting everywhere and crimes and misdemeanors in high places are creating a restless mood of frustration and lack of confidence in government, not to mention the erosion of faith in moral idealism. That the failure of governments to understand the law of rent and to collect the economic rent of land is at the bottom of our woes is seldom mentioned in the halls of learning, and is even less often mentioned by leaders in the church.

When the problem of starvation in various countries is discussed nothing is ever said, either in assemblies or in print, that might indicate an understanding of those basic and fundamental processes that are responsible for the fact of famine, nor is there apt to be any intelligent discussion as to why so many people are confronted with starvation. Of course, it will be said everywhere, there are "just too many people." Land and the necessity for its redistribution is often mentioned but only Georgists and those who believe in land value taxation understand how land could and should be redistributed, and every Georgist knows that the "just too many people" syndrome is pure bunk. A prominent India landowner recently worked hard to convince his fellow landowners that they should give up some of their land. It was a waste of time. Unless a proper land value tax is applied, any "voluntary land turnover" would have but temporary results. It is like the old cliche, "Redistribute the wealth so that everyone receives an equal amount and it will be just a matter of time until the wealth will have reverted to those who are the most shrewd and capable." That is only partly true. Unless those values which attach themselves to land are systematically captured by society in lieu of the taxes on commodities the owners of land will have captured the wealth for themselves.

If careful thinkers are agreed that there is far too much wealth in the hands of a few and that something should be done to redistribute wealth more equitably, why have those people who are so convinced not come up with some practical method whereby the gap might be closed? If anyone thinks the rich are going to surrender voluntarily an agreed-upon portion of their stocks and bonds—forget it! It will never happen, and even if it did, and we left the system to operate in the same old way, it would do no good in the long run. A

Communist takeover would do it but the cure would be worse than the disease. Total land value taxation would move in that direction and would reverse pressures and relieve tensions, but obviously the redistribution would not be instantaneous.

Those who initiated the income tax had high hopes that it would become an effective instrument in redistributing wealth. Many superficial thinkers can still be heard to say that the graduated income tax is the best kind of tax because it favors the poor and penalizes the rich. Aside from the fact that the rich have carved out tax shelters and have placed the burden of the tax on middle and upper-middle income people, and despite the further fact that many critics insist that we need only to eliminate the tax shelters to make the income tax respectable, we insist that even a graduated income tax does very little to redistribute the wealth. It still allows the law of rent to remain uncontrolled and that practically guarantees that rents will be high and commodities expensive. It will also guarantee that the margin of production will be very low and that, in consequence, the basic wage of labor will be far lower than is right or fair. Indeed, it has very little effect on the way the system works. If the government skims billions "off the top" and spreads them around, the ultimate result is that it increases rents and inflates land values. Indeed, the system will still be grinding out wealth for the few and poverty for the great majority. The income tax has enabled the government to collect and spend billions of dollars for both good and questionable purposes, but it certainly has not changed the money-flow materially. One thing it has surely accomplished; it has vastly added to the power of the Federal Government and along with the "patch and poultice" concept of government it has created a Frankenstein monster that is like the tail that wags the dog.

There is really only one way to redistribute wealth and to guarantee that it will not tend to clot automatically. In any country in the world where land is privately held, be it highly sophisticated or isolated and at the bottom of civilization's totem pole, the whole concept of land value taxation is designed to deal an effective blow at those practices which cause wealth to be inequitably distributed in the first place. Make land available to the common man anywhere and he will not starve. He may have a lot to learn, but with land at his disposal he will be in a position to play "catch-up-ball" with his fellows.Bad climatic conditions might wipe out the hoped for gains and even create some set-backs in spite of LVTaxation* but, under normal conditions, good results would follow. The rich would find it impossible to hold land out of use. Vigorous, imaginative and ambitious people would move in, everything would be spontaneous and, especially in the highly developed countries, our basic patterns of doing business would not be changed and everyone would

* LVT (land value taxation) sometimes LVTax or LVTaxation.

find his proper—not artificial—level in the scheme of things. Naturally, in a backward country, it would take some time before everything would be "up-to-date," as it is supposed to be in Kansas City, but meanwhile the people would not starve and the United States would not have to suffer from a guilt complex for allowing millions to die under famine conditions.

4

We are now in the throes of a brand of landownership the scope of which the world has hitherto never experienced. Say what you like about the Arab nations demanding exorbitant prices for their oil, the crux of the matter is that those who own the land in those countries are the government, and they have expanded their dreams of power by taking the landowners' position that says, "If you own the land where the richest deposits lie, there are almost no limits to your power. If the rest of the world must have what you possess, the price will be determined solely by their willingness to buy." It so happens that the industrially developed countries which have operated for centuries on that very policy, now find themselves in a terrible bind as the landowners of the Arab world are playing the old game of land monopoly and the people in the rest of the world, from personal experience, are finding out how it feels to be on the short end of things.

As technology advanced during the last two centuries the Western powers fanned out across the earth in search of raw materials, often using diplomatic power plays on under-developed countries in order to gain favorable concessions and unfair contracts. Sometimes, their negotiations were actually demands accompanied by threats of violence, all of which illustrates that there are other kinds of power than the kind that is exercised by landowners.

It is true that landowners in many under-developed countries had been content not to join the march of technological progress. They reasoned, "Why should we? We have everything we need and we can buy from the developed countries what they and their technology have produced. We have servants who work for pennies a day and multitudes who will do all the back-breaking work at subsistence wages. This will enable us to have all the money we need to satisfy our own wants and desires. Why should we worry about the desires of our tenants? If we invest capital in developing our own resources we would only have to follow the investments with the tasks of administration. Why should we take on such headaches when we have it made without doing anything?" So it was easier to pay others for their manufactured luxuries than to assume the tasks of developing their own resources.

But time marches on. The processes of development, as the superpowers moved in, brought added activity. Natives were hired to help man the projects and many people learned many new things. Eventually, the local landowners found the pressures mounting. Why not nationalize their holdings and cancel the previous arrangements, dismiss the foreigners and become their own developers? It need not oblige them to be much more generous with their own people as long as the owning cliques who made up the government ran the show. The ever-dependable law of rent would protect their own interests and keep the common people "common." Many Western technicians could be persuaded to stay on and eventually the local owners would exercise complete control. With such control they could demand higher prices, especially if the raw materials involved are scarce in other countries. This would be a way of enriching themselves by "upping" the rent.

This is why the Arabs are able to put a stranglehold on the Western World. They have the oil and they are able to produce it without too much foreign assistance. What they are asking in their increased prices is merely an increase in "rent" and the Western economies are placed in jeopardy. This is the stuff that wars are made of, and with atomic bombs and missiles in the offing we are all too poignantly aware that we must exercise extraordinary restraint. Something will have to give but if either business or political leaders begin talking out loud about the necessity of resorting to violent action, they can expect a public outcry the like of which they have never experienced before.

For sheer stupidity and utter madness there is nothing in the world to match the build-up of offensive and defensive weapons by Russia and the United States. Only our terrible fear of the awful consequences of atomic warfare is keeping either nation from asserting its national self-interest as disagreements surface. Never in history have human beings been so much in need of a body of law which could exercise restraints and fashion agreements amenable to all concerned. There is only one kind of bomb shelter that makes any sense in this crazy world. Whether we like it or not we are going to have to admit that international anarchy is a sleeping bomb that must be defused by the creation of a brand of world government that will effectively restrain the aggressions of power hungry nations. Despite persistent efforts of individuals and groups to bring such an organization into existence we are still searching for the means whereby dictatorships and democracies can be successfully merged. In a democracy the individual citizen is the "unit of power," but in a dictatorship, be it communist or fascist, all power is vested either in the official leaders of the state or the individual leader as the case might be. It would be relatively simple to draw up a constitution for a world government if all nations were practicing democracies, but the problem becomes almost hopelessly complicated when attempts are made to merge dictatorships and democracies. Consequently, without such a responsible body we are obliged to flounder about in the sea of power politics and we listen to reports that our

Secretary of State or our President has just committed us to "react in force" should aggression become intolerable. As time goes on, this brash stance begins to make us look ridiculous. We cannot continue to think of ourselves as the police force for the entire world.

Many Georgists I have known are convinced that the threat of wars will never cease until men in every country are agreed that "The Earth is the Lord's," and that all should have access to it on equal terms. Since a "single tax" on land value would, if intelligently instituted, allow the purposes of God to be accomplished so that men would "beat their swords into plowshares, and their spears into pruning hooks," many are convinced that a tax on land value should have priority. However, our international situation is too precarious, and the need for lawful restraints is too great for us to even think of waiting until we take care of the problem of landownership around the world. We have been depressingly unsuccessful in dealing with the problem in our own country and unless, and until, we demonstrate what a proper tax policy might do we can be certain that nothing significant is going to happen anywhere else. Tennyson's "Parliament of Man" was once but a poet's dream but today it has become a practical necessity and a matter of life or death for millions. If we cannot merge our legal powers we can at least make a far more effective instrument to deal with our recurring crises than the United Nations has provided.

One thing is certain in my own mind. Our political leaders will have to quit listening to the "big shots" in our business community and be considerably more inclined to use the United Nations in dealing with our international problems. When the chips are down and the headlines scream that we have reached a crisis we go running to the United Nations for cover. Weak as it is, the only world organization that we have could be infinitely more effective if we used it with proper respect. Moreover, it could be made much stronger if it were allowed to reflect the judgments of those who have no personal axes to grind.

CHAPTER SEVEN

# Dealing with the Law of Rent

Inasmuch as most Americans never even heard of the law of rent or, if they have, have never considered it as having any significant bearing on our current predicament, most concerned citizens, in discussing current problems, tend to flit from one hot topic to another, trying to decide what the government should do about this problem or that frightful crisis. Unless and until the majority of Americans get wise to the real cause of most of our multidudinous problems there will be nothing but frustration for any of us.

David Ricardo discovered the law of rent but it was Henry George who told us what to do about it. The only way to check its depredations is for the government to establish legal controls designed to keep landowners from appropriating "the excess of what can be produced on the best free land in use." We should simply base the tax solely on the annual rental value of land. Thus the state would appropriate the "excess" for itself in lieu of all taxes hitherto levied against labor products or labor itself. It has taken us two hundred years of malpractice to pile up our accumulation of closely related problems, and those who should have saved us from all these aggravations have failed us as thought organizers. Do we have to deal piecemeal with every problem that appears or can we make a basic adjustment that will of itself set many things to rights ?

## 2

Before moving on to explain exactly how we might effectively deal with the law of rent let us present a nut-shell statement of our basic thesis: Land always increases in value as society tends to populate certain areas. Reasons for these increases are that many individuals create institutions and services which make living in the community more desirable. As amenities are added in the form of roads, sewers, water systems, utilities, fire and police protection, schools, churches, libraries and all the governmental agencies which provide security and regulate business activity, the cumulative worth of all these things tends to attach itself to land and is reflected in the prices charged for the sale or rent of land. It seems reasonable to assume that since such values have been socially created, they should be socially collected and fairly distributed. Instead, they are pretty much expropriated by those who own the land. Whereupon, because society allows the landowners to profit by these values and fails to tax them properly for them, it becomes necessary to tax those whose efforts produced the wealth and made the community a more desirable place in which to live in the first place. It was the presence of all the socially created institutions and services which gave added value to land, and it most certainly was because such values were created that rents could be and were increased. Although many of those services were supplied by the government, many were supplied by the varied activities of many private citizens. No matter! Insofar as the activities of these others enhanced the value of the land, the landowners have traditionally claimed *all* the credit and have charged well for what they did not create.

Here lies the crux of most of our social problems. If there is a method whereby the people, in their capacity as a government, could appropriate a substantial part of that increased land value which we all helped to create, leaving for the landowner enough to make the ownership of land worthwhile, then it might be possible for the government to reduce, partially or wholly, the taxes on buildings and improvements. If this could be done, then all those who are holding land out of use for speculative reasons would be obliged either to put their land to profitable use or to get rid of it altogether, selling it to others who would so use it.

Before going on let us explain how the private collection of most of rent might be effectively checked. Very simply, the Georgist proposal involves a basic change in real estate tax policy. Instead of taxing land and buildings alike (as if they were alike!) and as if taxes did not produce opposite effects on each, it is proposed that the tax burden be shifted from buildings and improvements to land value. In other words, let land value be the sole base in the real estate tax. Given the present widespread state of ignorance regarding the effects that taxes have when based upon land value on the one hand or when based upon labor products on the other, and in the light of the consequent failure of state legislatures to provide the legal trackage for an enlightened tax policy, very few advocates of the Georgist doctrine believe it is realistic to assume that adoption of complete and total land value taxation in the nation is immediately possible. To be sure, Congress has the power to legislate tax policy in the nation. But having the legal right to do so and getting the job done are two entirely different things. Ideally, this is how it ought to be done and *must* be done as quickly as possible. Time is of the essence, and we are convinced that there is much less time left than most people are willing to admit.

Fortunately, there is one state in the nation where at least partial land value taxation is now legally possible. That state is Pennsylvania. A new law provides permissive legislation which allows city councils of forty-eight cities of the third class to base the city tax wholly or partially on land value. This means that city taxes that are now based on buildings could either be reduced or eliminated entirely. Please note that only city taxes could be so levied. School and county taxes have to be levied in the conventional manner.

We are now nearing the moment of truth. If what we have been saying about the law of rent is true, and if the law functions in such a way that far too much of the wealth produced from land or land sites is siphoned off into the coffers of landowners, it stands to reason that any method which would actually correct the money-flow would not be to the liking of those landowners who constitute the real "rip-off artists" in the mythical landowners' club. Under LVTaxation a great majority of homeowners would be immediately benefited by receiving lower tax bills. Vast numbers of people who own no land at all would enjoy lower rents. Even though these two groups make up the bulk of our population, those landowners who, because of the kinds of land investments that they have made, would receive higher tax bills, and for that reason alone would stir up so much opposition as to make its adoption by any city council very difficult. This will become crystal clear as we proceed.

3

So, here we go with a hypothetical, but realistic example. Let us take a town of 10,000 people and see what would happen. For the moment, we need not change the assessment process or introduce more scientific methods so as to guarantee equity and uniformity which should ideally be employed in preparing an assessment roll. Even though we may be convinced that assessment practices are not what they should be we can use the figures that we find on the assessment rolls of almost any American city. (Really, it matters little how large or how small our sample might be. The same general pattern will prevail in every case.) To be sure, land values and building values will have to be assessed separately. Our first concern will be to discover the grand totals of land and building values. Let us say that in our mythical city (not so mythical since it is modeled after a real town in Pennsylvania) the total of land values is $5,000,000 and of building values is $25,000,000, a ratio of 1 to 5. (It is absurd that there is such a difference as one goes from town to town. Sometimes the ratio is 1 to 2½, sometimes 1 to 3, and we even found one town where there were very few pretentious buildings at all but where the ratio was 1 to 7. All of which indicates that assessment practices are in a sorry state and that the government should insist upon all assessors being thoroughly trained in special schools so that we might have far more exact standards than now prevail.)

There are usually three taxing authorities in cities across the country. These base their taxes on property—the city, the school board and the county. Since all property taxes are based upon the combined value of land and buildings, in our sample city $30,000,000 will represent the tax base. Inasmuch as the city needs $300,000, a levy of 10 mills on $30,000,000 will yield that amount; the school board needs $360,000 and 12 mills will yield that amount; the county needs $120,000 and this will require a levy of four mills. Therefore, the total real estate tax will take an overall levy of 26 mills. This will raise $780,000. Inasmuch as we are proposing to base the property tax on land value *only* we will disregard building values. Since the city must have $300,000, a levy of 60 mills on $5,000,000 of land value will raise that amount; the school board must have $360,000 and a levy of 72 mills will be needed; the county must have $120,000 and a levy of 24 mills will be sufficient. The same amount of revenue, totalling $780,000, can then be raised with a total levy of 156 mills on land values alone. Having thus instituted the system we need only multiply the land value of each individual property by .156 in order to determine the amount of tax.

When we do this, some interesting things happen to tax bills. Since, in our example, the ratio of land to building values in the assessment is 1 to 5, the required tax will either be more or less than before, depending upon whether the ratio of land value to building value on each property is less or greater. Where the building value is exactly five times as much as the land value the tax will remain the same as under the present system. Example: The tax on a property with a land assessment of $1,500 and a building assessment of $7,500 would, under the current system, be $234.00 ($9,000 × .026). Under the LVTax system it would be just the same—$234.00 ($1,500 × .156). Most average properties with houses that are from twenty to forty years old would fall into this category. However, any improvements or additions to properties such as garages, blacktop driveways, new wings, or whatever, could now be made without incurring any additional assessment or tax. Therefore, any property owner who, at first, would seem to come out only even would actually be ahead of the game if he improved his property as he could then do without penalty.

Where the present building values are more than five times as great as the land values, the tax would be lower than before. Example: A property with a land assessment of $2,500 and a building assessment of $20,000 would presently call for a tax of $585.00 ($22,500 × .026). But the LVTax would be only $390.00 ($2,500 × .156). Even under the present unjust system people put their hearts and souls into their homes, and do not skimp, even though they know their taxes will be higher if they build good homes. But an LVTax system encourages people to build bigger and better homes and rewards them for doing so! Upper middle class people who like good homes should recognize this advantage. Too often, they are afraid that any tax that might be regarded as a "reform measure" would put them at a disadvantage. Not so! Builders of good homes are always rewarded when a tax is based upon land value.

Manufacturers, unless they operate in old dilapidated buildings, find that a land value tax will greatly reduce their tax. Sometimes the reduction is so great that it looks like a system set up especially to help them. An extreme example, due to the extensive plant equipment involved, can be cited. The Hammermill Paper Company in Erie would save approximately $160,000 annually under a land value tax system. On city taxes alone it would have saved $62,000, but when in 1964 this was brought to the attention of their then treasurer he scoffed and said it was just so much chicken feed. We doubt if the present treasurer would feel that way. In case anyone might conclude that a LVTax would help manufacturers more than they might deserve, let him remember that they are the ones who provide most of the jobs and that to cripple them is to cripple those who are eager and anxious to produce. Moreover, that mysteriously wonderful open market will take over and in a strictly egalitarian society it plays no favorites. Whatever advantages manufacturers might have enjoyed in the days before labor unions came into existence have been pretty well neutralized. It is quite obvious that labor unions have established their gains in this sector and we are not recommending that they forfeit their gains in the hope of enjoying the benefits of land value taxation. No way!

Those enterprises which are obliged to invest heavily in buildings will always benefit under LVTaxation. We have in mind mortuaries and banks, hi-rise motels, apartments and office buildings. This is as it should be because such people have made heavy investments of their capital and have improved the areas in which they operate. They have, in doing so, increased the value of their neighbors' land and do not deserve to be penalized for having done so. An LVTax system would provide incentives for the building of fine apartment buildings within walking distance of the central city area, thus contributing to a solution of the transportation problem in our cities.

## 4

We come now to that aspect of land value taxation which arouses so much opposition. Landowners have been taking unfair advantage of the real producers of wealth for centuries. It does not matter what kind of land might be involved, whether agricultural, commercial, recreational, or land for domestic purposes. The hard fact is that our conventional tax policy of taxing land and buildings alike and usually assessing land at a lighter rate than that of buildings, has set the stage in America for a multibillion dollar rip-off by which land speculators siphon off vast quantities of wealth and drastically interfere with the just and even flow of wealth from those who produce it to those who do not earn it or deserve it. They simply draw their wealth from values that accrue to their land by the efforts of others.

As we continue to examine the trends and pressures which a total land value tax policy would engender it will become increasingly clear why the suggestion of a land value tax policy is bound to arouse the ire of particular classes of landowners. Those who own and use their land are always immediately benefited. From such, the proponents of a land value tax system get very little flak. However, those who buy and sell land with no intention of using it for any social good usually find that a land value tax is detrimental to their immediate self-interest. As we present our description of what is sure to happen to certain kinds of land investments, no one need be surprised if the whole idea proves obnoxious to 1) those who hold on to large tracts of land as a future personal preserve or 2) those who own vacant lots or undeveloped tracts of land in or near the outskirts of a city or 3) those who own important sites in the high rent districts of central city areas, which sites have obsolete buildings that are seventy-five or one hundred years old and which long since have paid for themselves or 4) those who make a business of buying and holding land for future development and using certain income tax benefits to off-set the low taxes on their vacant land as it appreciates in value. In contrast, homeowners who live in their homes are the "good guys" in our catalogue of landowners. They almost always keep their properties in first class condition and would find that a LVTax would reward them handsomely by giving them lower tax bills.

But, under land value taxation, what would happen to those who might be called the "bad guys" in the landowners' club? They may not really be bad guys at all! They may only be doing what any shrewd businessman would do under our inequitable system. Let us take for an example a slumlord who owns property located a short distance from the central business district. Because it is "close in" and potentially valuable, the land assessment is $3,000 while an old beat-up house is assessed at $2,000. Under the conventional system his tax would be $130.00 (5,000 × .026) but his LVTax would be $468.00 (3,000 × .156). Most people do not realize it but slumlords always figure on making from 20 to 40 percent annually and often get their principal back in three or four years. This is because they seldom improve their properties. Tens of thousands of people in America (some frustrated beyond all imagination) own old buildings located on "close-in" and therefore potentially valuable land, but they cannot afford to raze the old buildings and build anew the type and size of buildings which would be appropriate to the locations. The present high tax on buildings would make such an investment unprofitable. However, under LVTaxation, suitable buildings could be built and rented at profitable figures. Obsolescence and decay would gradually give way to handsome and well appointed buildings, not only in downtown areas but in all parts of the city.

Again consider the thousands of owners of very valuable land sites in the central city districts of America. Our observation would indicate that about 95% of such owners would suffer an immediate tax increase should LVTaxation be instituted. Usually their buildings are obsolete and even ramshackle. In many instances their land values would be higher than their building values and that is certainly worse than a ratio of 1 to 5. Main Street, America, is famous for its red brick mausoleums and dingy walk-ups. But why blame the owners of central city properties who have taken the line of least resistance? In view of the high tax that would be levied against any new construction, and because, under the present tax system, advantageous locations permit landowners to demand exorbitant rents despite the wretched condition of the buildings, they elect to continue to collect heavy ground rents rather than to invest capital in new buildings and so incur much heavier tax bills.

For example, in our mythical city there is a five-and-dime emporium two stories high but with ample floor space and well located. The building has paid for itself long since, but it still has "use value." There are four apartments on the second floor, all occupied. With land assessed at $40,000 and the building at $30,000 the current tax is $1,820 ($70,000 × .026). Usually, the annual rent being charged for such buildings is a deep, dark secret. The owner, the renter and the lawyer know but they won't tell. Currently, assessors use the possible selling price of a property as a guide in determining a fair estimate of its value, so it is important that sale prices become matters of public record. A few recorded sales up and down the street is about all an assessor has to help him with the assessment. The store manager (sympathetic to our cause) leaked the information that his company was paying $1,100 per month rent or $13,200 annually, a figure which exceeds the tax he is obligated to pay by $11,380. If the state were to collect a proper share of the rent that "excess" would no longer go to the landowner but to the community as a whole in lieu of the far too burdensome taxes being levied against houses and manufacturing plants where building values are greatly in excess of the land values which homeowners and industries use. After all, was it not the presence and activity of all the people in the community which created the rental value of land in the first place?

But let someone whisper to him that they are talking about switching taxes from buildings to land value; that his tax on the following year would be $6,240 instead of $1,820; and that he could not recoup his loss by raising rents. Then he might bestir himself and take the first plane back to Homeville to see what could be done about whoever started this "nonsense" about land value taxation! A whole local army of legal "rip-off-artists" would descend upon the city council. Talk about a can of worms! Is it any wonder that those who own the properties along Main Street in America, along with those who own most of the run-down rented properties in town, are opposed to land value taxation? These are the people who are making the most of our conventional tax policy and taking in rent the wealth that is actually being produced by those who work in the buildings of the high rent districts of America. The only reason we put up with it is that the people "just don't understand."

Unfortunately our present tax policy enables owners of central city sites to collect high rents for properties equipped with antiquated buildings. Most of the owners will oppose the institution of LVTaxation. Paradoxically, the very system which they would oppose would enable them to build fine, new, rentable buildings which would be a delight to themselves and all their fellow citizens.

There is another group, perhaps not quite so influential as owners of central city sites but quite numerous, who will object strenuously to the institution of land value taxation. They are the owners of vacant lots or holders of vacant areas where new developments are bound to occur. Currently, in all American cities, vacant lots are gingerly treated by assessors. A lot that might easily sell for $10,000 is often assessed at only $2,000. In our model city the tax would be $52.00, but the LVTax would be $312.00. The owner would not be too badly hurt because what a LVTax takes away with one hand it gives back generously with the other. A new building can now be erected without the threat of a punishing tax. What is truly wonderful is that it could be a really fine home or business building and no tax at all would be levied against the building. Owners of land which is being held for development could go ahead and build far better homes than they might have dared do prior to the adoption of land value taxation. To the extent that they are mere speculators with no intention of using the land they will be out-and-out losers and naturally they will fight any effort to institute LVTaxation. Make no mistake, this evil and unjust situation cannot be corrected without those who have been the spoilers becoming livid with anger. Naturally! No real reform could ever be instituted without angering those who have been "cashing in unjustly" on the conventional system.

## 5

We come now to the most important aspect of the whole idea—the energizing of the economy of any community that has the wit to adopt land value taxation. We have pointed out how taxes on buildings hinder the whole building process, and how low taxes on land value make the price of land high. These are the two prongs of a gigantic pincer movement that is holding progress back all over America. You find a town that needs a good inner-city motel. There is a site beautifully located for such a venture. You inquire about the price of the land. It is headachingly high. Already you are discouraged, but you go to the assessor and ask, "What would my taxes be on a multistory motel worth two million dollars?" The answer finds you holding your aching head in your hands and leaving town. It happens everywhere. We are imprisoned by the high price of land and the high cost of buildings.

Correct this condition; let any city knock the price of land down by collecting the public revenue from the rental value of land; stop taxing buildings, and as many other products of human labor as possible, and a famous advertising slogan, "Progress is our most important product" will become an "all-American" watchword.

If such a tax policy were instituted there would develop such a stir in the economy of a city as to focus the attention of the entire nation on the amazing results. A building boom would ensue; old run-down properties would give way to great stores, office and apartment buildings, modern factories and beautiful homes. A flood of new enterprises would be drawn to the community as if by a magnet. Building materials and builders of all kinds would be in demand. Hundreds would come running. News that buildings could be erected without paying any tax on building value would spread like wildfire. Land, long vacant, could be bought at greatly reduced prices. Beautiful buildings for all purposes would replace the mausoleums and dingy walk-ups. The whole city would become an architect's dream. Firms, looking for places to build factories, apartments, warehouses, or whatever, would come running and the Chamber of Commerce would be deluged with inquiries.

These facts should have been known by the time this country was being settled. However, no one had as yet appeared to explain the differing effects of taxing land value on the one hand and that of taxing labor products such as buildings on the other. The terrible conditions in Europe, from which the early settlers of this country fled, were caused primarily by the failure of governments to deal with the law of rent. A relatively few scholars and the important landowners must have understood but they preferred to keep things the way they were. Most of those who emigrated to America thought the vexations of European life could be voted away by giving the ballot to the common man. They did not understand that it was the refusal to tax land value and the subsequent clotting of economic power that was at the bottom of all the deviltry in Europe. This fact has remained obscure to most Americans even to this day. Our lack of understanding has nurtured a multibillion dollar, non-productive business which, though perfectly legal, had all the effects of an underworld racket in that it preyed on the people who produced wealth by robbing them of the fruits of their labor.

No one can blame people for taking advantage of a tax policy that enables them to reap where they have not sown! Because of the enormous influence of a relatively few people who have made the kinds of investments that have enabled them to put a tap on so much of the wealth that has been produced, those of us who understand how they get away with it have been rendered powerless. These "wrong kinds of investors" not only collect big and easy money, but they guard the citadels of their power by constantly bringing pressure to bear upon every potential source of information, using the schools, the churches and the media to make sure that their secret weapons are never exposed.

How else can one explain the almost total lack of any public mention of the basic facts that our thesis sets forth? We Georgists talk to ourselves all the time. A veritable intellectual feast is spread upon my own desk constantly, but only on the rarest of occasions can we persuade newspapers or magazines to publish the no-holds-barred kind of material that we are exchanging with one another. Very few legislators seem to know what should be done. In fact very few people have been brought to a point of understanding that it is our fallacious method of taxing real estate that is at the bottom of so great a stream of injustices. Most people have assumed that our plight is the natural result of the increase of population (pure nonsense) and the introduction of scientific inventions (utter hogwash). We repeat: one hundred men can produce much, much more wealth than ten times as much as ten men can produce, and how could one imagine that a machine that is manned by one man who can produce a thousand times as much wealth per day as one man could have produced two hundred years ago, can do anything but vastly increase the supply of wealth. The American people need to know how the people as a whole, and not a relatively few super-wealthy landowners, can become the beneficiaries of the marvelous train of technical discoveries and inventions to which we should all have fallen heir.

Had a land value tax policy prevailed from the beginning our cities would have been built out evenly. The thirteen million vacant lots in the cities of America would nearly all be in use. There would have been no suburban sprawl caused by leap-frogging tactics as people went farther and farther out into rural areas where they could buy land cheap, leaving vast areas lying idle between the city and the far-out suburban developments. Our local governments and utility agencies would have avoided the waste involved in running roads, sewers, telephone, gas and electric lines past endless miles of undeveloped areas. Endless hours of time would have been saved by millions who are now obliged to commute daily past wide expanses of vacant land.

What is even more intriguing, the obsolescence and decay that has settled down upon our cities could, and would, have been avoided. Instead of dingy rows of old worn-out buildings desecrating our cities we might all be justifyably proud of the quality and attractiveness of the buildings in all sections of our cities.

Total and complete land value taxation, scientifically administered, would not change the basic business procedures with which we are all familiar, but it would so revolutionize our economy as seemingly to change our life-style. The change would be in the direction of a far more equitable distribution of wealth. In adopting such a tax policy we would simulate the conditions that prevailed in our society for many years before our failure to tax land values had produced the present artificial scarcity of land. In those days there was no unemployment and little sympathy for those who did not work. Crime was almost non-existent and one could walk the streets at night without fear. Houses were large enough so that children of aged parents could easily take care of them when their working days were over. Work opportunities were plentiful so that even people of limited strength could contribute to their own upkeep and so ease the burden of their care in their last days. There was very little need for government welfare programs, and private social institutions assumed responsibility for dealing with those personal emergencies that cannot always be avoided in this world.

CHAPTER EIGHT

# So What Good Would That Do?

This was my own reaction when I asked who Henry George was and what it was that he recommended. The answer was all so different from the usual run of suggested reforms. Norman Thomas and Stuart Chase were trying desperately to put it all together back in 1931. Neither they nor any of the other popular writers ever mentioned the significance of land. If they ever heard of the law of rent they certainly gave it no credence. If the cover was complete at the time of the great depression, it is even more so today. There were then, and still are, thousands of people, both in and out of the churches, who regard themselves as socially concerned but who haven't the ghost of an idea where all the trouble is coming from.

We all know about business cycles, but seldom do writers realize that in such a cycle land values and prices keep going up, and up, and up, and at last — precipitously down. This invariably happens, eventually. It has been some forty years since the bottom dropped out of land prices. The last to give in are the landowners. Their capitulation usually signals an upturn. In the thirties recovery was sluggish and things did not pick up until we began contracting for weapons to be used, first by Europeans and later by our own country. Any system that has to depend upon periodic wars to keep it functioning is desperately in need of being overhauled. The business cycle, back in the eighteen hundreds, came full circle in just a few years. For many reasons our economy has not really "hit bottom" since the early thirties and land has not been fully depreciated. Recessions became the mode and before things got too bad the demand for many highly desirable things such as electric utilities, radios, television sets and automobiles which brought on a whole train of related activity such as highway construction, sales agencies, gas stations and garages, kept the economy moving along. There were periods when land prices did fall some and real estate was slow but up until the present combination of unemployment and inflation, along with the complications brought on by the oil crisis, we have managed to pick up the pieces and move forward. But now, the scene has changed. The people want no part of another war and the establishment "big-wigs" want no part of a basic economic reform. The people are ill-informed as to what a basic reform might entail and here we all are, sweating it out, with young people losing their faith in a possible future and millions of unemployed growing more and more desperate, and with many on the lower levels of society losing their grip on the verities of life and becoming ripe prey to all kinds of moral turpitude.

If we were to begin an analysis of the business cycle and were to start at the point where the price of all kinds of land has at last come down, so that those who could afford to buy or rent it could organize some productive or useful enterprise, we would note that the most significant result of the increased business activity would be the steady rise in the prices and rents demanded for land. Owners may not have rendered any service to justify their demands, nor are the demands due entirely to cupidity. The plain fact is — they know they can get it. They may not understand why, but they know they always have — and so think of it as their natural right. With a business venture about to get underway, the confidence of its organizers prompts them to pay more for the land than they might like, but hope springs eternal, and they go ahead anyway. Without land they are helpless, and with land the owners are in a position to demand more than it is really worth. All landowners have a way of sticking together. They all belong to the most powerful union in the world. They have no organization and they need no recognized leader. Everyone just follows the principle — get all you can and look sharp to see how much your fellow-landowner is asking. As business picks up, always keep increasing the rent, never forgetting that yours is a strategic position. What you have has a monopoly aspect and sooner or later you can get your price.

As the cycle continues upward, with business getting better and banks relaxing their credit restrictions, everything conspires to increase the value of land. There is no basic reason for this other than that monopoly aspect which landownership conveys. Certainly, nothing a landowner has done justifies his increased demand for higher rent.* He knows he is in the driver's seat and can always "cut himself in" on the proceeds of the business. All owners know this and they all act accordingly, always keeping ahead of the game. It is so much a part of the scheme of things that no individual landowner need think of himself as a rascal. What he is asking is the "going rent," just as what the laborers are getting is the "going wage." Both are closely related. Long before the public becomes aware of a general inflationary trend, this systematic inflation of land values is laying the foundation for things to come. Prior to a crash, hastened along by the "hope eternal," all producers are tempted to overreach themselves. Even the cautious bankers make loans for land purchases that are not justified. Always the landowners keep inching up their demands until the price of land is so high that by sheer compulsion men are compelled to pull back.

* When we speak of land we mean *land*, not the combination of land and buildings. Often higher maintenance costs, higher costs of materials for improvements and higher taxes on buildings will impel owners to increase what is mistakenly called "rent."

## 2

So what good would land value taxation do? For starters, it would wipe out the advantages which enable landowners to "cut themselves in" on the earnings of others. More and more of the rents we pay to landowners would go to the government, and more of the taxes, now based on commodities, could be rescinded. Less and less government subsidies would be needed; more and more people would be profitably employed; with high grades of land now being made more easily available, those with ideas and with what it takes to carry them out would become employers; and if the assessors would do their work right and quit listening to landowners, there would be more jobs than people to fill them. Naturally, the rich would scream their heads off, but what would be happening to them would be infinitely better than being liquidated in a communist takeover. As for the rest of us, it would be far better than a fascist coup which is what the rich will try—and probably manage—to engineer.

Continuing to address ourselves to the question, "So what good would that do?" we come to that aspect of land value taxation which is apt to turn many superficial thinkers off. To suggest a policy that would knock the price of all land down will strike most property owners as an irresponsible act of social suicide. We have all been conditioned to think that when land prices are going up everything is roses. Not so! Sooner or later the time will come when all land will be so high that few can afford to buy it. What then? — recession, unemployment, business failures, accumulated agonies in families of lower and middle income people, increased welfare costs, crime in the streets and drug abuse to dull the pain of living. If we really are socially concerned we must resist this "propaganda ploy" of the landowning class and rejoice when land prices come down.

## 3

Everyone instinctively realizes that land is all-important. Any suggested change that would seem to threaten the iron-clad right to own land (and to be protected in the right to all the benefits that owning valuable land has always brought) is automatically suspect. When it is suggested that we should adopt a tax policy that would reduce the price of land, cold shivers run up the backs of all those who own any land at all. We have all been so conditioned to the conventional ways of doing things that any official act that would reduce the price of land, and especially our land, would seem to be an abdication of the powers-that-be in protecting us in our holdings. Such a reaction may well be justified if the land in question is being held out of use for speculative purposes. But the reaction is completely illogical if the land is being *used* and the owner is not being compelled to pay taxes for his improvements.

One fact that is always covered up and never mentioned in modern economic lore is that a no-tax or a low-tax policy on land value inevitably creates an artificial scarcity of land, and the concept of scarcity is an important one in economic thought. In the first chapter of his book, *Economics and the Public Purpose*,* John Kenneth Galbraith quotes two definitions of economics—one by Lionel Robbins: "The science which studies human behavior as a relationship between ends and scarce means which have alternative uses." The other by Paul A. Samuelson: "How . . . we choose to use scarce productive resources with alternative uses, to meet proscribed ends . . ." Being accustomed to using the straightforward statement that economics is the study which deals with the production and distribution of wealth in human society, I thought at first that he was kidding. Then, it dawned upon me that he was serious. For all their concern about the significance of "scarce productive resources" you never hear any of them speak of the way our conventional tax policies work to create *artificial* scarcity of land for the purpose of enriching those in control of land at the expense of those who are not in control.

If the conventional economists were truly interested in identifying those things that are really scarce, they would have to frankly announce that high land prices are not the result of scarcity of land but the direct result of society's failure to tax land value and thus to appropriate the socially created values reflected in the price of land. Land may be too scarce to gratify the limitless desires of all the people in the world, but there is enough land in America to maintain a population twice as large as we now have. Ecologically, we would have problems, but today, much of what may look like scarcity is purely artificial because of our low tax policy on land value.

There are some natural resources that we have recklessly used up. One cannot help thinking of the oil that was wasted in shuttling some 500,000 men to and from Viet Nam, and of the millions of gallons of gasoline it took to blanket that country's enemies with bombs dropped from planes that had to be flown from 500 to 1500 miles to and from the targets. This certainly will have to be reckoned with as a real and deliberately induced scarcity. But the artificial scarcity of land, brought about by our failure to tax land properly, is something else. The waste involved in our failure to use the potential energy in arable land, and the economic loss to the nation in supporting a system that prevents millions of people from producing, making it necessary for society to provide them with the means of life, strikes us as proof that we are all being unbelievably obtuse and hanging on the precipice of sheer madness.

* Page 4.

# 4

Moreover, we have also been viciously conditioned to see "good" when we hear that so-and-so has just made a killing in land. For example, an interstate highway is carved through some forsaken area of woodland and hills. Those lucky owners of land where interchanges occur—land that was not worth a nickel before—is now sold to motel builders or gas companies for thousands of dollars. To be sure, the windfall is more than welcome, but for society as a whole it means that so many more thousands of dollars have "gone to rent"—dollars that might better have been channeled back into the system to repay those who invested the capital and labor that produced the highway, the motels and the gas stations. Again, we hear of some farmer whose grandfather happened to buy a farm near a city. Time passes and the land is needed for residential development. Result: what may have cost the grandfather a hard earned five thousand is now sold to a big developer for $150,000. We have been conditioned to rejoice in the good fortune of the grandson, but with this happening on the edges of thousands of towns and cities across the land, if all those billions had been channeled back into the system to repay those who had provided the capital and done the work, none of those recipients of pure "rent" would have needed the windfall in the first place. Literally trillions of dollars have been "going to rent," most of which is retained by private owners, as millions of such deals have been consummated. We say, "Let society as a whole be the beneficiaries and we will all be better off."

Most people will embrace any method by which they might legally lay claim to windfalls. They will applaud those who have been suddenly enriched by winning a state lottery. It may surprise many such people for us to say that the universal enjoyment of windfalls, due to land speculation, has mightily contributed to our moral delinquency. As long as it is legal, we tend to look upon any method whereby we might come into great wealth as both just and proper. We are not in the mood to condemn inheritances but it certainly is true that many lives have been ruined by them, just the same. Religious people who reject the practice of betting on the races, playing slot machines or investing in state lotteries will happily embrace any opportunity to make a bundle in some land deal. They would reject any argument that would put their taking of such a windfall into the same category as a big day at the races. Nevertheless, the comparison is logical, even though its universality and legal justification have almost totally obscured the fact that it is morally indefensible. Good church people who wouldn't buy a lottery ticket or even turn up at the race track will vote to dismiss a minister if he pushes too hard for land value taxation. That, I know, only too well!

5

In this chapter we are thinking (theoretically) of the dividends that might accrue if we could institute "total and complete" land value taxation. When the inevitable restraints of multiple taxes on labor products are removed and all those tax pressures become tax incentives, the subsequent increase in production will automatically raise land values everywhere. Unless the "doctors of society" can skillfully channel those increases in land value into the public treasury and reduce or rescind taxes on commodities, and/or on labor and earned incomes, any effort to make it "total and complete" and to keep it that way will fail. In order to do this all assessors will have to shift their mental gears and learn to base the tax upon annual rental value rather than upon the selling price of land.

This concept is crucial. Under a land value tax system all assessors will have to focus all their attention on the *annual rental value* of land. This, and not the selling price, must be regarded as the tax base. To say that it is impossible to determine what the annual rental value of a particular land site might be is to deny that buyers of land ever did know what they were doing. Men have been buying land for centuries and the appraising business has its own precise standards. Anyone who says it is impossible to appraise the true value of land simply doesn't know what he is talking about. Mistakes are bound to occur if appraisers do not know their business, but good appraisers can skillfully pinpoint the value of land. Business sites are constantly coming up for review as leases expire and have to be renewed. The market is active and constantly at work. Under our current system the landowner can often afford to hold out for a higher rent or price, whereas under a land value tax system he would be under strong pressure to deal more quickly.

Landowners have been very close-mouthed about the sales prices or rents that they have been getting. In order to assist appraisers and assessors many states have passed laws, making it mandatory that selling prices be made matters of public record. Assessors can, with a fair degree of accuracy, figure what the rental value of land is simply by using the conventional method of fixing land prices. Thus, by making annual rental values matters of public record, the chances of error in estimating the tax would be greatly reduced. Appraisers and assessors would not have to depend upon a few scattered sales. They would have current information on every site along a street to guide them. Thus, their judgments would be very reliable.

Both those who favor, and those who are opposed to, land value taxation stumble over an aspect of the mechanics involved in instituting the tax. Upon hearing that a LVTax will reduce the selling price of land, and assuming that the tax is going to be based upon selling price, they say, "It stands to reason that as the selling price goes down, as per an agreed upon schedule, that with each successive fall in the price it will be necessary for the assessor to increase the millage year after year in order to raise the desired revenue. When, finally, the price of the land reaches zero then even one million mills times zero will still be zero." "Therefore," they say, "how are you going to implement such a tax?"

Obviously, the answer is that the selling price of any piece of land would depend upon the amount of the rental value which at any given time might be taken by the government in taxes. If 90% of the annual rental earning is going to the tax authorities and only 10% is being kept by the individual owner, the price, which is what the buyer is obliged to pay to the landowner to secure legal title, will be only 10% as high as it would have been had the state levied no tax at all. This does not mean that the ultimate user will be paying less rent than before. It means that a large part of what he once paid as rent to the landlord is now going to the government which is taking most of the rent but calling it a tax. Actually, the government is collecting the "economic rent" in lieu of taxes on buildings. The rent fund remains the same but the tax fund is greatly reduced when there is a building on the land. The better the building the greater will be the tax saving. Moreover, the tax on the increased land value would be much lower than the tax that would have been required because of the new building. Many landowners have bought land and held it out of use and undeveloped while others improved adjacent properties. Then, when others had invested heavily in building up the area, they were able to command fabulous prices for their undeveloped land because of the investments made by others. Land value taxation would make such an unfair ripoff impossible.

## 6

Anyone who elects to advocate land value taxation in a city will soon discover that his most determined opposition will come from the owners of choice sites in the high rent districts. Naturally! They are the ones who are cashing in big at the expense of those who work long hours in buildings that are obsolete. Those who have improved their land by erecting modern and highly useful buildings raise no objections at all. But they are relatively few in number. Our conventional tax policy has made it extremely difficult for landowners in the downtown areas to improve their land properly. The imposition of a high tax on buildings has compelled landowners to take the easy route by taking advantage of the strategic location of their land and demanding excessively high rents for the use of buildings that are literally ramshackle. To them, at first, the idea of switching to LVTaxation is abhorrent, but with taxes on buildings rescinded they can profitably invest in a new building. Indeed, because their properties are strategically located and are high in potential usefulness, they can take advantage of the no-tax policy on buildings and build respectable monuments to themselves, right in the middle of their own hometowns. There it would be "The John Smith Building," or whatever, emblazoned in granite for their friends—and everyone else—to see. It would certainly beat the "madness" of our using tax funds in a futile effort to stem the tide of obsolescence now rampant in all of our cities.

Let anyone who is willing to press the case for LVTaxation be aware that owners of choice commercial locations have been subjected to a whole set of fallacious policies which have influenced them to adopt inhuman attitudes. Our upside-down tax policy has made them what many of them are. They know that what they have is potentially very valuable and their determination to get the most they can in rent is perfectly natural. Unfortunately, the system makes them act like rogues. One principle is always followed. Never give a hard-working or talented renter an even break. If you are not careful in demanding the highest possible rent, you can easily lose your silk shirt, and that might turn out to be a ten thousand dollar rag. If you lease your property to some ordinary looking character and he turns out to be a wizard at merchandizing, and if you have not taken the precaution to include an escalator clause in the contract so as to "cut yourself in" on his superior ability, you might turn out "a cropper." All you can do is to chide yourself because you had the upper hand all along and just plain failed to use it.

Downtown properties are extremely valuable. Compared to residential sites the differences in value are sometimes unbelievable. Naturally, the owners of downtown sites are never "casual" in selecting their tenants and their returns are sometimes fabulous. The fact that the rents which they collect are "unearned" and represent the monopoly aspect of choice commercial land sites never bothers them. They have been getting away with their fat returns for years and are not about to stand by and watch their special privileges evaporate into thin air. Consequently, although there might be only one thousand such landowners in a city whose taxes will be raised under LVTaxation, and fifty thousand homeowners (including themselves, if they still happen to live in town) whose taxes will be substantially reduced and whose right to improve their properties without any additional tax will be guaranteed by law, those one thousand owners of downtown properties will have ten times as much influence at City Hall as the fifty thousand owners of good homes across the city, Take our word for it. We know!

# 7

Assuming that we were suddenly able to overcome our blindness and institute all at once a system of "total and complete" land value taxation, all those who had made the wrong kinds of investments in land would have to change their ways, If they had been deliberately holding good land out of use in the hope of making an unearned profit, with no desire or intention to use the land themselves, they would have to get rid of their land. Or, if they did not wish to sell, they could keep it and use it if they were willing to do something with it. With the money they got for selling it they could buy just as much and just as good land somewhere else, but there would be no point in doing so unless they wanted to use it. From the time that the land value tax system was instituted all land contracts would have to be changed to take into account the new arrangements. If a person had agreed to pay $10,000 for a lot and was doing so systematically, and all of a sudden the lot was reduced in price to $2,000, there should be a provision in the law that would allow the buyer to pay on a reduced scale.. Landowners would object strenuously but they could buy elsewhere at the reduced rate themselves. There would be no injustice to the seller and no real loss to the buyer. If the buyer had just paid cash for his $10,000 lot and suddenly discovered that he would have to move to another city or to another part of town, only to discover that his lot was now, under LVTaxation, worth only $2,000, he need not panic. He could buy another erstwhile $10,000 lot for $2,000 somewhere else. What difference would it make? Actually he has gained the right to improve his lot without tax penalty and this was more than he had bargained for under the old system. No one need shed any tears over his predicament for he is actually better off than he was before. If he had already built a fine home on the lot his future taxes would be less than before and because of this, coupled with the lower costs of daily living that would follow the rescinding of multiple taxes on labor products, he would find his situation much better than before.

So much for what would happen to the average homeowner should "total and complete" LVTaxation become tax policy. How would it affect the super-rich? We mentioned in a previous chapter that the builders (capitalists, not landowners) of the Socony-Mobil building in New York, 42nd Street and Lexington Avenue, were allegedly paying owners of the land $500,000 "rent" annually. In this instance landowners and capitalists or builders are not the same. If the annual rental fee for the land alone is $500,000 and the government is planning to take 90% of the annual rental value, the landowner who will then have to be satisfied with 10% of the rental value, would receive only $50,000. Currently, because he receives $500,000 in rent he would ask $10,000,000 in a sale ($500,000 × 20—capitalized at 5%). Under LVT he could ask only $1,000,000 ($50,000 × 20). Naturally, this would quite decisively clip the wings of the landowner and enormously benefit the capitalists and the builders. This is as it should be. Again, let us remind the reader that the landowner can pick up another property with his $1,000,000 should he elect to sell. He could get just as good a property for that amount anywhere. There would be no point in his doing so unless he wanted to use it himself. If he did want to use it he could build a wonderful building on it without tax penalty? So what has he really lost? He has lost an enormous "unearned income" and society as a whole will have benefited because in that one instance $450,000 will have been plowed back into the system. Otherwise it would all have "gone to rent." Is it any wonder New York is in trouble?

Most people can work up a tearful sympathy for the disadvantaged rich but remain utterly oblivious to the plight of millions who have no jobs at which to work and no decent place in which to live. The super-rich might be inconvenienced but not improvished. The options of holders of too much land would be infinitely better than the options of millions who have nothing and not even a chance of getting anything. The plight of a few hundred thousand people who would have to shift their investments, compared to the plight of millions who have nothing, would hardly bring anything but crocodile tears to the eyes of a sensitive onlooker. Very few wealthy people have all their money invested in land. Most of them have substantial holdings in stocks and bonds. All they would have to do would be to change their investment policies and under LVTaxation they would discover a veritable gold mine in collecting interest or earnings on capital rather than collecting unearned rent on land.

## 8

Anyone who suspects that a switch to land value taxation might throw our economic mechanism out of balance should realize that our present taxing system tends to obstruct and hinder production all along the line. When a tax makes land, the basic source of all wealth, expensive and artificially scarce, allowing those who are financially strong to collect more than their proper share of production, the overall effect is negative. Taxes create pressures and the pressures that our present tax policies create are all negative. Land is hard to come by and everyone is penalized by the state for producing,—a fine (?) way for a presumably democratic state to behave! If the system were to be suddenly and completely changed so that all kinds of land were made easily accessible to all who needed them and wanted to use them, and if the restraining and punitive influence of taxes were done away with by simply rescinding the taxes on commodities and all labor products, all the pressures would become positive. If all of the industries in America were to find themselves freed from repressive taxes, how in the name of common sense could the overall effects be bad for the economy as a whole? Many adjustments would have to be made. Laws affecting land tenure and mortgage payments would have to be changed, but if one is thinking in terms of getting the economy moving, all adjustments would be for the good.

Let us list briefly some of the things that would happen if we were to adopt total and complete land value taxation. They would not happen instantaneously. It would take time, but within five years after its adoption this country would be a showcase for the rest of the world to ponder. One thing *would* happen instantaneously. If it could be done rapidly, everyone would be able to find work and that in itself would serve to breathe life and hope into our shattered dreams of what America ought to be. Relief programs already in existence need not be rescinded until it became obvious that they were no longer needed. The people could be encouraged to "hang in there" until the real benefits were being developed by the application of all kinds of labor to all kinds of land.

When full and complete LVTaxation had become a reality these are some of the things that would certainly occur. Roughly, we would estimate that at least 80% of all homeowners would enjoy substantial tax reductions. 2) About 95% of all manufacturing plants would also enjoy large tax reductions, and these could encourage employment and reduce the prices of their goods. 3) A building boom would ensue as new houses could be built tax free on land that had been reduced in price. 4) Vacant areas in cities would be improved. 5) Every family would reconsider where and how it might now afford to live, and many would plan to move up to better land areas. 6) That extensive area of blight that now marks the section adjacent to the central city and extending out, sometimes as far as five miles, would begin to be rebuilt. (Clevelanders may think of Superior and St. Clair Avenues out as far as the University; Buffalonians may think of those one hundred year old buildings all around the downtown area; Philadelphians may think of those *dozens of square miles* of row houses visible on both sides of the elevated both west and north of the central city; Chicagoans may think of those terrible buildings along the elevated tracks in all directions toward the suburbs.) Every city in America has its centers of decay and all of these would vanish within a period of five or ten years. 7) All American cities are losing substantial taxpayers who are fleeing to the suburbs. This migration can be quickly reversed as new and attractive apartments are erected so that thousands can walk to their places of employment. 8) Owners of old buildings, now being abandoned, could tear them down and build fine rentable buildings in their places.

We predict that if ever the American people come to their senses and quit throwing up road-blocks to impede progress, that every segment of society will be made stronger. We would get the land speculators off our backs and the millions of owners of very valuable land sites would have to quit jacking up the rents just because they know they can get away with it. Thus, billions of dollars would find their way into the economic bloodstream. Indeed, under such an arrangement, we predict that in a very few years we could wipe out the entire national debt—something which the defenders of the *status quo* have given up all hope of ever accomplishing.

One of the dividends of LVTaxation for society as a whole is that, when properly instituted, no one will either make or lose money by merely buying and selling land. Obviously, those who now make huge profits by buying, selling and renting land will abhor such a prospect. But it does have its points. Never again would any individual be swindled by some run-away land boom. The eliminating of land speculators would keep a lot of thieving schemers honest. They would be obliged to apply their talents to something constructive. No longer would anyone suffer because an unforeseen set of circumstances caused his land to lose its value. With the loss of annual rental value the tax would automatically be reduced. Conversely, land in a favorable location would call for a continually rising tax as long as the value goes up. In this way no landowner would benefit by the combined actions of civic or social agencies, and no inactive individual could cash in on the accomplishments of productive people whose activities resulted in higher land values.

After all, doesn't it make sense to say that when a man produces something of worth, or renders some service that others are willing to pay for, that what he produces and what he receives for his service should entitle him to command and enjoy the benefits of his labor. He would be protected in his ownership of those things and all manufactured goods that society and the free market says he should have. If production and service rendered are the basic requirements for possession of wealth, how can anyone logically justify exclusive ownership of something which neither he nor anyone else has created?

Land is God-given, and when the Scriptures say, "The earth is the Lord's" the inference is that it is God's gift to *all* of His children. In a democracy, land, which is the source of all wealth, should be regarded as the common heritage of all, and if anyone thinks this is "socialism" it is proof-positive that someone has been tampering with his brain cells. In some circles they would call it "brain-washing!" If a great thinker and a marvelously humane spirit like Henry George comes along after five thousand years of confused thinking and twisted logic, all of which has resulted in horrible examples of exploitation and devastating wars, and explains in fine detail how a modern society can engineer its social order so that the gifts of creation can be equitably distributed, why are we so slow of wit and fearful of spirit not to embrace all of its blessed prospects?

CHAPTER NINE

# When the True Remedy Is Rejected

A healthy system of wealth distribution in any society, whether agrarian or industrial, is obviously essential to its well-being. If there are no points in the system where individuals or corporations can legally claim more than a just share in the wealth produced, the distribution process will be equitable. But if some arbitrary rule or practice prevails which interrupts the even flow at any particular point, then whenever the money which represents the wealth reaches that point, the whole scheme of things will be thrown out of balance and the free and open market will no longer operate accurately. Moreover, the imbalance will be aggravated every time the money-flow reaches that point as it makes its way around the system. Our thesis is that the one basic point where maldistribution exists in any society which practices private ownership of land is that point at which men pay for land use. Here the law is "rigged" in favor of the landowner, so that every time rent is paid for the use of land, or every time a higher than proper price is paid for the purchase of land—from that point on, there is less and less wealth available to those who use the land.

It is because of the above unfair and repetitive process that the smooth flow of money is interfered with and one person or corporation is permitted to take more than is just or fair. In due time, as 'round and 'round the money goes, areas of "money famine" appear. When, in a modern democracy, a famine develops in some sector of the economy, the government is called upon to grant a subsidy. But this cannot effect a cure. It can give only temporary relief. The basic cause of the maladjustment has not been corrected. Had it not been for the misdirected money-flow in the first place there would have been no famine to treat. But, with things as they are, famine areas grow more and more numerous as time goes on, and as long as nothing is done to correct the system at the usual key point where the flow of wealth is misdirected, the overall conditions grow progressively worse.

Once such an unbalanced money-flow system has become traditional, enjoying acceptance and status in society, the process of wealth distribution enriches those who own important land sites and another kind of reaction begins to show up in the economic process. Once the original process is looked upon as being right by all members of society, even though it is not right at all, and once its daily functioning causes wealth to clot in the hands of one segment of society, there is a natural economic reflex (perhaps we should call it a human reflex) which shows up in criminal activity, schemingly clever undercover deals, out and out bribery and both business and political corruption. When the basic processes of wealth distribution are not fair, it becomes very difficult for society to control the activities of those whose moral and social restraints are less than ideal.

Very early in this game the super-rich landowners subvert the talents of able and clever people by hiring them to oversee and manage their affairs. They hire skilled professionals to lobby at state and federal levels of government; they make attractive contributions to election campaigns for which they expect favors in return; they hire clever people to plot and scheme in their behalf so that they can take advantage of further investment opportunities. Indeed, most of the really sound and potentially profitable opportunities fall into their laps because they have the means to organize and oversee the processes of production.

In the later stages of the game when the system has gone almost to its extreme limits, and the concentration of wealth has created vast pockets of need; when all kinds of businesses have failed and unemployment has mounted everywhere, the schemers and plotters will have become so thoroughly established in the scheme of things as to make it appear that they supply basic economic necessities, and that without their superior expertise we would all be worse off than we are. The simple fact is that much of what happens in those latter stages of economic ill-being would never have happened at all if we ordinary folk had had the wit to deal intelligently with the law of rent. Had we done so, the clever administrators, the able accountants and the army of subservient lawyers would all be busily and happily working for themselves and the variety of their economic activities would be unbelievably numerous.

## 2

At the risk of being redundant, let us say that our difficulty goes back to the almost universal error of failing to distinguish between land and labor products. No matter how complicated the system might be, there is no way that, given a free market, the money-flow will prove faulty at any other point than at that which is made plain by an understanding of the law of rent. Neither is there any way that *laissez-faire* can guarantee wholeness and well-being when most of the land and wealth has been captured by the few.

The so-called liberals and "new economics" majors who do not realize where the real difficulty is, often argue that if we could just get the arms race under control so that billions could be diverted from costly weaponry to such things as housing for the poor, libraries and colleges for the intellectually hungry, transportation systems for energy conservation and as many other social needs as social idealists might conjure up, we could turn the whole thing around and everything would be smooth and prosperous. Most liberals think this an appealing idea and find no flaw in it, except that it would prove an almost impossible achievement at this point in time, due to our failure to create a body of law to supplant our present methods of power politics and negotiated settlements. Much as we might thrill to such a proposition and much as we would like to believe that—in our collective capacity under the guise of government of, by and for the people—we might collect vast sums, channel them through government bureaus and allot them grandiosely to this or that needful area, thus enriching our common lives beyond all imagining, we have to declare that this would be no way to deal with our problem. Everything that would happen that would appear to be good would result in the increase of land values, and those who were in a position to collect the consequent increased rents would be the ultimate winners. What this age needs is another Newton to explain how "economic gravity" operates wherever the law of rent goes uncontrolled.

Perhaps what this age needs more than anything else is for America to show the people in other parts of the world how to deal with their economic problems. Can you imagine the guilt complexes that would develop in our minds if we were to spend for domestic needs the money which is now going for armament, while the rest of the world is starving and the bloated stomachs of children are being shown on our television sets? If so, how could we live with our common-people-affluence? One thing Georgists have believed for decades is that once land is made available to people they will take care of themselves and that regardless of the so-called level of development that might prevail in particular areas—all they really need is *land*. There is nothing static or limited in supply about better ideas, better methods and better tools. Once the people are free to use the land, they can survive until the better ways of life can be achieved. Meanwhile, to contend that America must gird itself to be the breadbasket for the world is beyond all reason. Not that we would denigrate the motives of charity but that we would emphasize that worldwide injustice has created such huge pockets of famine as cannot be dealt with by anything short of basic reform. In today's world the needs of charity have long since outrun the resources of the charitable.

Refusal either to understand or to deal intelligently with our problem has created pockets of poverty here ever since Europeans came to America. Still, it was so much better here than in Europe, thanks to the abundance of free land, that we did not realize that we had never really managed to get out of the old groove. When, at last, the finite supplies of land in America became artificially scarce and began to cost much more, the pockets of poverty began to surface.

3

There are two kinds of power available whereby we can deal with human need—1) social power and 2) state power. When needs arise and citizens, apart from government, respond to the need, raising and administering funds and using voluntary help, they are using social power. Money is thereby redistributed from those who have to those who have not. In our land, for well over two hundred years, social power was used almost exclusively to meet human need. Churches and private charitable institutions responded to such limited needs as did exist. Prior to the great depression there was only a limited amount of state power used to deal with the needs of the indigent and crisis-ridden poor. But, at the inception of the New Deal, poverty conditions had become so wide-spread, and the private social-power-agencies became so swamped with appeals for help that the Federal Government of necessity moved in. From that time on state power began to supplant social power. Although social power still operates on a fairly large scale and United Catholic, Protestant, Jewish and Community Funds continue to meet many of the marginal needs of the poor and unfortunate, the great bulk of help, extended to those in need today, is supplied by state power. Now that the income tax enjoys such a huge take the government not only makes millions available to failing businesses but it is obliged to maintain a welfare program which, although necessary under the circumstances, tends to destroy the initiative of the poor and do inestimable damage to the work ethic. If current funds run dry there is always the printing press and more inflation!

4

Late in the 19th century, labor unions developed their own new and unique ways of "redistributing" the wealth. They used pressure tactics and were able to bring pressure to bear upon "owners" (not managers, since managers merely do the will of the owners) to secure better wages. In those early days of labor union activity there was little chance of success unless the corporations involved were very large and dependent upon large numbers of skilled and highly trained personnel. Railroads were among the first to succumb to labor union pressure. Later, with the New Deal in full swing and with public sentiment moving toward a more sympathetic attitide, labor unions were granted a higher degree of legal support and out-and-out pressure tactics gave way to collective bargaining methods. Large manufacturing concerns became targets and the power of labor organizations increased mightily. In a sense the efforts of organized labor did tend to wrest from owners moneys that would otherwise have been appropriated by them. In a very real sense the increased wages represented what might be called a redistribution of wealth, and those involved were able to enjoy the products of their own hands—something which laborers had been denied for centuries. However, the labor unions have provided very little relief for well over 70% of the labor force who could not organize, and millions of people are still limited in their power to command reasonable wages. The law of rent still has its way with that segment of society.

It becomes increasingly clear that as long as we go on our present merry way to destruction the greater becomes the need for government to make huge grants to bail out large segments of our economy, and to just keep alive millions of unemployed and indigent people. It should give us pause that so many of our citizens are just barely getting by, and that we have a normal expectancy that 4% of our people will be unemployed even when times are at their best. Under depression conditions that figure could rise to 10% and more. This is intolerable and could well be disastrous as millions are thrown out of work and businesses are failing everywhere.

The pity of it is, that should the economy "come back," so that 4% would be unemployed and everyone would cheer, still millions would be unable to find jobs and more millions in urban ghettos and country slums would just barely be getting by. Heartbreaking situations would still prevail everywhere. Millions of dollars worth of wealth would remain unproduced, making us all poorer than we otherwise might be, but any desire to effect a cure would be lost because everyone believes that all is back to normal, quite oblivious to the fact that there might be such a thing as a system in which free enterprise was still the mode, and at the same time where full employment was a reality.

In chapter three (Diametrically Opposite Effects) we dealt with the first principle of taxation, namely, that taxes on land value can never be passed on while taxes on labor products are always passed on and paid by the consumer at the end of the line. We also explained why a tax policy consistent with those basic facts would automatically correct many abuses now rampant in our economy. We will now go on to make what might appear to the not-yet-quite-convinced reader a few seemingly strong claims which have been part of the philosophy of Georgists for years. In short, our thesis is: that any and all previous efforts—such as trying to increase wages for labor by organizing labor unions, or attempting to redistribute wealth by instituting the graduated income tax, or attempting to ameliorate conditions in this or that ailing segment of the economy by empowering bureaucrats to use extensive governmental grants and subsidies—actually effect no really *basic* changes, and in the long run, are only abortive. Moreover, when some reform that does tend to improve conditions is instituted, the inevitable result is that land values are increased and since no change in the tax policy has been made to channel the increased rent fund into the public revenue stream, the result is merely to increase the rent-take on the part of those landowners who are always in line to benefit by increased land values. This is the normal and inevitable effect of all such correctives. As long as the government, which is "us," does not change the scale of taxes on land value the landowners can sit back and smile complaisantly, knowing that they will be the ultimate beneficiaries of any palliative measures taken.

In our varied efforts to deal with whatever economic woes have developed we have not only failed to increase the tax on land values but we have persisted in using labor products as tax bases, which practice also tends to increase land values and eventually to increase the rent-take on the part of the fortunate landowners. Thus all taxes on labor products produce accumulated negative effects. By taxing commodities we penalize ourselves for getting up in the morning and going to work; by taxing people for making deals (sales), without which we could not exchange what we have produced for what others have to sell, we discourage economic give-and-take; by taxing incomes in a low-land-value-tax economy we maximize confusion by failing to distinguish between earned and unearned income and lumping them both into one category; by taxing capital gains under the guise of being tough on "big shots," all we do is to add to the taxes on labor products because all capital is merely a form of labor production; and by taxing labor itself we are saying to one another that anyone who works should be punished—up to a point. So all these negative approaches, coupled with the additional negative practice of taxing commodities instead of land value, increases the rent-take for landowners. In all this we really do foul up the economic process!

With all this going on and while land value goes almost scot-free from taxation we have stubbornly refused to deal objectively with our real problem. By our stubbornness we have allowed millions of acres of farm land and millions of city lots and vacant areas to be held out of production or use, forcing the margin of production to lower and lower levels and thus automatically keeping the wage level for ordinary, unskilled labor far below what it justly ought to be. Meanwhile we have made the price of land far too high and have priced many labor products beyond the reach of millions. We have applied brakes to our economy while motors are everywhere available. There are a lot of things that are done in this world that make no sense at all, but this process tops them all for a clear case of social madness.

Consider for a moment organized labor. We would not deny for a moment that *all* labor should be better paid. This is the essential element in our basic thesis. It was our failure to control the law of rent that made the conditions of labor so intolerable for centuries. Anyone who has studied the long, hard struggle of those involved in the labor movement, and anyone who has any knowledge of how desperate the conditions of the working classes have been, cannot criticize or deride those who have worked so desperately to bring about changes. However, such gains as have been chalked up could never have been achieved had it not been for two very significant things, namely, 1) the discovery and settlement of the Western Hemisphere and 2) the industrial revolution. Had there been no "new world" beckoning to the disinherited of Europe, resulting in economic opportunities never before experienced, and had there not developed large industrial plants which were vulnerable when labor unions finally dared to strike, the death-grip of aristocratic landowners would still be a major fact of western culture.

However, much as we may glory in the gains made by labor unions, and much as we appreciate that by demanding a reasonable share in production they actually created markets for the goods that they produced and gave new life and power to the economy, it still remains a fact that much of their gain has been swallowed up by those who buy and sell land for profit. Everything that happened sent land values higher and higher. Laboring people, always eager to own their own homes and now in a position to buy land, found the price of land steadily going up. Those who were not organized were obliged to pay higher rents. For some who were organized it was better than a stand-off and the rewards were well worth the effort, despite the fact that they were obliged to borrow heavily and to pay interest for twenty or thirty years in order to own the high-priced land. But those who were not organized were the losers and were condemned to struggle along with very little hope of ever owning their own homes.

Labor leaders may justly argue that, had they waited for those who advocated land value taxation to achieve it, they would still be working at marginal wages. We admit the charge, but now that we must either adopt a new tax policy or watch our civilization disintegrate, we implore all workers and producers (and this includes executives and managers, because their interests are not and never really were those of the landowners) to move for the kind of action that will benefit *all* labor. Concessions, once gained, need not be revoked. Labor, having won its position by great effort, really has nothing to fear from a progressive application of land value taxation.

## 5

Consider now the effects of the graduated income tax. Let us begin by declaring that any act on the part of the government to put money into circulation by taking excessive amounts of wealth from the rich and giving it to the poor, may be salutary—up to a point. However, it is no way to deal with the basic problem of maldistribution. In the first place, it does not change the process by which the rich got that way. When the income tax was instituted it was hoped that it would tend to cancel the evil effects of the maldistribution of wealth. Had this been true, you may be sure the recommendation would have been met with more opposition than it did. The super-rich would have thrown all their considerable influence into a campaign to defeat it. Although an income tax was not entirely to their liking they knew that they could live with it as long as the institution of private ownership of land was not disturbed, and as long as land and buildings were taxed alike—as if they were alike! If, because of the income tax, conditions generally were better, land values would be increased and they could at least partially recoup by simply upping the rents.

Woodrow Wilson, in whose administration the income tax was instituted, was familiar with, and looked with favor upon the philosophy of Henry George, but he did not realize how the income tax could be corrupted. Certainly he never suspected that it would grow to such proportions as it has. If he were living today he would be horrified. The tax shelters, so cunningly set up; the overall temptation to cheat; the loss in productive manpower caused by the vast army of clerks, accountants and tax specialists; and the excessive power of the federal government to grant its largess to local authorities—all these would have sent him reeling. There is no doubt that the graduated income tax has sent money moving through the system, as huge grants were made to rescue this or that ailing segment of the economy—ailments that need never have occurred had the tax system been right to begin with.

## 6

We have all become so accustomed to having the government respond to appeals for help to bolster up broken down businesses, inadequately-financed state programs, and even threats of communist take-overs in scattered parts of the world that we overlook the strains that such giveaways and low-interest loans have on the value of the dollar. Whether we get the money from the varied tax funds or sell bonds and add to the national debt, the effect is the same. It is no wonder that a wide breach has developed between conservatives and so-called liberals. Since neither group understands where the trouble has originated and most people assume that one must be more right than the other, it is little wonder that we fumble along with temporary palliatives. The English unashamedly refer to it as "muddling."

There comes a time when all such programs fail to produce sizable waves of economic activity, so that many landowners receive very little benefit. That time seems to have arrived. Let me quote from a letter which appeared in the New York Times (3-6-75) which reflects the reaction of a conservative to the effects of the colossal giveaway programs of the past thirty years.

"I can understand conservatives now being critical; many times having warned us of the inevitable result of the brutal abuse of our economic system. But many of those who are most indignant about it are the very ones who foredoomed us to it by their irresponsible advocacy of excessive spending.

"The biggest causes of our problems are long continued, astronomical government deficits and unjustified wage increases. But few politicians have the guts to say so because that isn't a good way to get re-elected.

"These liberal critics have the effrontery to tell us how to solve our problems. Where were they when the country was adopting more and more spending programs? Where were they when business was under unbearable pressure from unions and government to grant wage increases not justified by productivity? Where were they when enormously expensive social programs were adopted, although it was obvious that, no matter how desirable, they could not be afforded all at once?

"Anyone who criticized such proposals were loudly accused of placing considerations of property ahead of human rights. He was scorned by so-called 'concerned' people, who assumed that they, as the sole possessors of compassion, were entitled to a blank check against inexhaustible funds. Their utter lack of responsibility has brought economic tragedy to millions of the people they sought to help."

Here we have the brand of reasoning that characterizes most conservatives. As far as they go, they are right. But, like most conservatives, this individual reveals no understanding of the facts which we have been emphasizing. He would probably scorn anyone who tried to explain that our entire tax system is fallacious and that our whole economic system is a carry-over from the days of feudalism. He would probably contend that the poor are poor because they have no talent in the art of making money.

On the other hand, those who have been responsible for irresponsible spending will deny the allegation and recommend more spending to get us out of the predicament in which we now find ourselves. Most of them are so conditioned to think in activistic terms that they simply cannot take the idea of land value taxation seriously. "Oh yes," they will say, "a change in the tax system might have a superficial effect for the better." But for anyone to claim that land value taxation would turn things around is, to them, sheer nonsense. Never having made a careful and exhaustive study of all the angles they simply cannot believe it could be a viable solution.

To suggest to conservatives that our real estate tax policy is to blame for our present predicament, and to suggest to liberals that all of their correctives are mere palliatives and, in the long run, only make matters worse because they tend to increase land values, is for both groups just too, too far out. Both conservatives and liberals will wriggle and writhe to get off of this absurd hook, but we are convinced that unless, and until, we take strong steps in the direction of land value taxation we are in for a long, dark night of trouble.

So, here we are, sailing our ship of thought between the Scylla of tradition-ridden conservatism and the Charybdis of compassionate liberalism. Yes, liberal with government funds, they certainly are, but liberal in the sense of wanting to see everyone on a free and equal basis—hardly. And here we are in the middle, with both conservatives and liberals thinking we are 'way out in left field because they cannot believe that our economic problems are mostly problems in taxation. Conservatives will turn away and refuse to give our ideas brain-room because they do not respond warmly to their less aristocratic implications. Liberals, although liking to think of themselves as open minded, just cannot accept the idea that all we have to do is to make the game of life fair at the beginning and then let things take care of themselves. As a young graduate of my own college, upon insisting that I give him in one sentence what I thought should be done about our economy, explosively replied, "Aw no! It will have to be something much more dramatic than that!"

CHAPTER TEN

# Synthetic Economics—The Best of Two Worlds

Anyone who would argue that what we have been saying is relatively inconsequential is really saying that all taxes now being imposed in countries where land is privately held are themselves inconsequential. Even the ideologically deaf, mute and blind cannot deny that there is a widespread outcry against our real estate taxes. Homeowners everywhere are not only crying, they are screaming. Feelings are running so high that superficial thinkers are saying, "Let us be rid of real estate taxes altogether." Nothing could be more damaging to the welfare of the common man than to adopt such a policy. It would eliminate, once and for all, the only method whereby our vexatious tax problems could be solved. Such an error in judgment would never have been expressed if our schools had not failed to instruct us in the elemental principles of taxation. The fact that so few people are disturbed when it is suggested that we eliminate real estate taxes proves how little people really understand about taxes and what should or should not be taxed. In the face of all the complaints we hear about taxes, seldom will anyone mention the really dual character of real estate and point out that when we tax buildings and improvements we are taxing labor products, and that to do so is bound to make them more expensive, while when we tax those values that attach themselves to land itself we bring the price of land down and make much vacant and unused land available to those who need it. Is there anything that any of us need any more?

When some high level politician or would-be statesman recommends that we should declare a reduction of taxes in order to stimulate the economy and get the unemployed back to work, he proves that he also has no real understanding of our basic tax problem. The saving in taxes might have a salutary effect and start money flowing through the system, but no *basic* benefit will accrue, for in order to replace the money forfeited by the government it will be necessary for the government to borrow and so increase the national debt. In 1974 we paid out over thirty billion dollars to service the national debt. The end result of a tax reduction would be that somehow, sometime, that money will have to be repaid. All along we have been trying to point out that most of our taxes tend to discourage production because they are actually penalties for producing in the first place. If our political leaders understood the first principles of taxation they would know that by increasing taxes on land value and decreasing the taxes on buildings and improvements there would be an immediate increase in economic activity. Moreover, there would be no sad day of reckoning because no borrowing would be necessary. But as it is, things may get worse and worse but there will be no public official who will risk his political neck by recommending such a sensible action. The people themselves are going to have to understand this before their elected officials will dare to come to their rescue.

## 2

Every country in the "free world" functions with economies and social systems that came into being long before anyone understood there was such a thing as the law of rent, or that it was persistently at work. In most countries governments never levy any tax at all on land value, and even today where land is taxed lightly, customs and traditions established under such naked landlordism still prevail. And so, where there has never developed a public outcry, forcing a government to ease the burdens of the disinherited, social conditions have become unbelievably deplorable. Wherever the so-called "new economics" (Socialism, Labor Party, The New Deal) has brought its ameliorating provisions the very relief engendered has resulted in complicating the picture, making the effects of the uncontrolled law of rent more obscure and seemingly less vicious and more tolerable. If there are any among our readers who are still unconvinced that it is necessary to put controls on the law of rent instead of running to the government and demanding more bureaus which must be supported by raising more taxes along the conventional lines, consider that a continuation of such a policy will most certainly socialize our entire economy. This might not be the worst thing in the world if it were not for the doleful fact that when crises arise socialistic regimes almost invariably slip into fascist dictatorships, and along with such a calamity will go all our vaunted liberties, making our lives a constant trial, where all that is left for freedom-loving men is to "wail and gnash their teeth," and all the while, carefully avoid being heard or seen.

As we all know, in recent years the "new economics" theorists have been riding high in the highly developed countries, but the wealth still clots, the great fortunes still increase in magnitude, and the big companies crowd out or swallow up small independent businesses, so that the ownership and control of our economy becomes concentrated in fewer and fewer hands. Even the conservatives, despite their theoretical disapproval, have felt compelled to adopt many of the "new economics" provisions. Since they, too, do not know what is actually causing most of our troubles, they go along with those who *claim* they do understand. However, thoughtful conservatives do point out that the proponents of the new economics (perhaps we should call it "governomics") proceed on the blatant assumption of the communists that there is no God, and since some men are smarter than other men, the smart ones have the responsibility to look after those who are "dull of wit."

It has always puzzled those of us who were raised on a diet of religious idealism how godless people were going to come up with a godly world. Seemingly, the conservatives would just as soon leave God out of the picture. At least, that is what they tell their ministers. Conservative ministers do not have to be told—they agree. Although the communists impolitely bow God out of their universe, eliminating troublesome clergymen in the process, the conservatives prefer to believe that as long as men are honest, reliable and true to the high ideals of service that God, in his mysterious ways, will bring it all together and hold it firm. The French had a secular name for those mysterious processes. They called it "*laissez faire*."

Although both communists and traditionalists seem to be embarrassed by the idea that God has an overwhelming interest in economics, they both agree that "goodness" cannot be left out of the picture. The traditionalists would limit their goodness to such virtues as trust, industry, thrift, reliability and eagerness to be of service. To be sure, in the overall pattern of things, their practices might eventually cause bitter suffering and bring premature death to millions, but at least they do not openly and deliberately espouse frank lying and premeditated murder—or do they? (Shades of those covert activities of the C.I.A.!) On the other hand, the communists may, with great compassion, redistribute the wealth and give food and shelter to the destitute, but they prefer to choose with careful deliberation to whom they will lie and whom they will choose to murder. Understandably, neither seem to want to become too openly involved with God. They might feel obliged to behave!

Even though proponents of the new economics have given up on *laissez faire*, insisting that in our modern world it is virtually bankrupt and that something in the machinery has jammed, making it no longer valid, conservatives are loath to admit this and still insist upon believing in its mysterious ways. They are both wrong. Those mysterious processes could be made to work, even in our modern industrial world, if only we had the wit to put proper controls on the law of rent. Our forebears inadvertently failed to deal with the law of rent and brought on such an ungodly state of inequity as to throw everything out of balance. *Laissez faire* can do the mysterious things of God only when basic justice (God) has been admitted into the system.

Georgists everywhere still accept the validity of *laissez faire*. Whether they choose to identify it with "the mysterious processes of God" is beside the point. After all, Georgists are recruited from the ranks of Catholics, Protestants, Jews and, yes, those who claim no religious affiliation at all. For all that, their economic views tend to bring them together and to cultivate among them a sense of mutual appreciation. They know that, given a proper setting (i.e. an adequately controlled law of rent, resulting in an equitable distribution of wealth), the processes of the law of supply and demand and the amazing automations of the open market would usher in a new day of social justice in which many of our mountainous social headaches would become as molehills.

3

We have been living for centuries, and still live, within the framework of uncontrolled landlordism. The sophisticates of our day often refer to feudalism and imply that it no longer exists, now that it has been supplanted by capitalism. This is rubbish! Capitalism, as we know it, is "feudalism complicated." The same uncontrolled law of rent that brought untold misery to millions is still at work, threatening the very peace and welfare of today's millions. We continue to be propagandized to go out and fight to protect the interests of those who own the earth, and because we have been so skillfully misinformed many will be gullible enough or will feel compelled to "fall in line" despite the atomic weapons and their horrible prospects.

In many countries of the Western World the new ecomomics has brought its easements, but the basic processes of the law of rent have never been properly and fully controlled in any country—anywhere. Here and there across the world partial controls have been applied. The most successful are those in Australia and New Zealand. Although the amount of land value taxation applied in those countries has been pitifully inadequate the results have been convincingly beneficial. In many cities of those countries buildings are completely exempt. However, real estate taxes are comparatively light because such revenues are not used to support the educational system as they are in the United States. Remarkable results have been obtained in Johannesburg, South Africa. Pictures of cities where even partial controls have been applied reveal that there is a solid build-up across the cities with very few vacant lots and very few buildings that are obsolete. Two Pennsylvania cities, Pittsburgh and Scranton, have had what we choose to call "slivers" of land value taxation for many years. The results, especially in Pittsburgh, have been amazing. Assessors in Pittsburgh understood how to take advantage of the tax and, long before the Federal Government came up with urban renewal programs, the leaders in Pittsburgh were able to change what was virtually a slum area into what is known today as The Golden Triangle. Partial controls were applied in Denmark, Western Canada and in some scattered local areas; but, by and large, the "free world" has eschewed any and all thoroughgoing controls because the rich and powerful will have none of it, and they do get their way in this world most of the time.

Because of our misunderstanding and consequent malpractice, which results from our failure to distinguish betweeen God-given land and man-made products, comes a whole train of evil consequences. For the same reason that wealth clotted in pre-industrial England, it also tends to clot in a modern industrial society. Indeed the tempo is accelerated. It was especially so in America where people of unusual drive and ability managed to apply their skills in developing hitherto unheard of businesses. Not that it is ever a lead-pipe cinch for some individual or group to put it all together, but once the combination of a great idea and the talent of some outstanding administrator team up and get under way the law of rent begins to play into their hands. Everyone knows that money, if wisely handled, certainly does make the making of money easy, and once a money-maker's business begins to "fly" he experiences the thrill of being propelled by a powerful tail-wind. The unseen forces of the law of rent will be undergirding his every effort. Just as there are brilliant and unusual musicians, clever and convincing politicians, eloquent preachers, and skillful writers, there are individuals with a gift for making money, and for them nothing succeeds like success. Our whole system is geared to stifle the less able and thus the maldistribution of wealth is accelerated. We have no desire to level everyone down to a common plane, but in the realm of economic behavior we are convinced that a proper control of the law of rent would enable many more people to get into the act.

John Kenneth Galbraith* admits that the unequal distribution of our wealth is a real problem in that a relatively few enormous corporations are able to cut themselves free from open market competition and can fix prices in compliance with other firms. He admits this is not healthy but since reform is not his chief concern, it remains only an unpleasant fact. He says, "An assembly of the heads of the firms doing half of all the business in the United States would, except in appearance, be unimpressive in a university auditorium and nearly invisible in the stadium."

In a footnote on the same page he quotes Professor William F. Mueller as saying, "There exists an extremely asymmetrical industrial structure, with the bulk of economic (i.e., industrial) activity controlled by an elite of a few hundred enormous corporations and the remainder divided among four hundred thousand small and medium-sized (manufacturing) businesses." In other words, whereas the "elite" could be contained in a normal sized au-

**Economics and the Public Purpose*—p. 43.

ditorium, it would take several stadiums to accommodate the heads of all the small manufacturing companies.

This unequal distribution of wealth is without question our most aggravating problem. While LVTaxation might prove no instant cure-all, yet full and complete taxation of land values and a subsequent reduction of taxes on all buildings and improvements would so energize the economy, and throw open so many doors of opportunity for the "do-ers" in society, that we could almost disregard the need for a redistribution of the wealth. Indeed, the very process would turn the money-flow around and gradually bring about a change in the methods of investment being employed by the super-rich. Instead of putting their money into land and thus putting much high-grade land beyond the reach of the do-ers, they would put their money into capital investments and by that very process start the gummed-up wheels of industry into motion.

## 4

Students of economics in these times are led to believe that there are only two basic forms of social organization. One is popularly, but mistakenly, called Capitalism, the other, popularly, but mistakenly, called Communism. Since each system was named by advocates of the other system the names convey certain elements of contempt and suggestions of reproach. The dominant power of "big money" and its rough-shod way of dealing with human beings is captured in the concept known as Capitalism. The all-powerful will of the ruling clique and of its dictatorial authoritarianism is captured in the concept known as Communism. The Marxist critic of capitalism looks beyond the democratic governmental forms and sees only the ruthless acts of the "money barons." Those who are critical of the Marxist ideology feel that all the boasted sense of happy acquiescence and voluntary cooperation of a truly communal type of organization is wiped out by the all-powerful will of the ruling clique which pulls the levers behind a front of communal action.

In basic theory, though not in actual fact, those who support the so-called capitalistic system, assert that *the individual* should enjoy the rights and benefits of ownership of both land and labor products. The communists, on the other hand, insist that all such rights of ownership should be vested in *the State*. In actual fact, neither is consistent. In America, for instance, by virtue of a tax system of long standing, the individual is denied exclusive ownership of either land or labor products, the government claiming the right to collect whatever portions of either land or labor products it deems necessary for the support of all its service agencies. On the other hand, the Soviet government apportions only a small part of the wealth to individuals, keeping most of it for its own use as a state. In either system the individual is denied the full fruit of his labor.

Now that we have carefully pointed up the distinction between land and labor products it might be safe to declare that both systems, capitalism and communism, are at fault. We say "safe" because without such a distinction clearly in mind, most readers would react negatively to what we are about to declare. In *neither* of the two systems is there any clear-cut effort to distinguish between the nature of land and that of labor products. This becomes lethal as time goes on because each system has within itself the seeds of ultimate failure. Capitalism will fail because it does not guard against "gross inequity," so that eventually absolute power is granted to those who own most of the land and who, consequently, control the means of production. Communism will fail because reckless and omnipotent power is granted to the state, giving it control not only of the land and of all natural resources but even of all the means of production and of all labor products.

These approaches are both essentially wrong. While the rights of ownership must be protected by law, let those rights accrue only to beneficial production. When an individual or a firm produces anything that has exchange value, the ownership of whatever is so produced should be vested in that individual or firm. Whatever a man produces, on condition that he has paid a just rent or price for the land which he might have used, should be his to keep, to sell, or to give away as he might choose. This is really the only just criterion upon which to base the concept of ownership, and we should respect and protect the rights of all owners to enjoy what they have produced without let or hindrance or even sales tax. Note that our limiting phrase, *on condition that he has paid a just rent*, is the crux of the matter. This is absolutely basic. There is no justification for a government to violate the citizen's basic right of ownership, except in cases of extreme emergency. In instituting a tax policy, we insist that a government should keep its "cotton pickin' fingers" out of the pockets of the people. What is even more imperative, let a government see to it that none are obliged to pay rent for land other than to the government itself. After all, it is the government that provides the services, not some free-lance landowner, and it is the people themselves who actually create the values which attach themselves to land. If we are not wise in determining how that "just rent" is to be arrived at, or who is to receive it, there can be no effective resolution of our social problem.

To make that statement is to make most Christians I have known florid-faced with sudden anger. "What's that you are saying? Are you implying that we should socialize the land?" But in their very asking of that question they indict themselves. They reveal that they do not understand the basic difference between land and labor products. By collecting 90% of the annual rental value of all land and, in doing so, rescinding taxes on most labor products we could de-socialize almost everything else. The land should belong to all the people, not to just a few. Socialism is just as guilty of confusing the nature of land and social products as are the proponents of capitalism and communism. Unless we see clearly that those values which attach themselves to land, having been created by 1) the pressure of population, 2) improvements in the arts of production, and 3) refinements in the arts of government, are actually socially created values that should be appropriated by society for all to enjoy; and unless we recognize that a government has no moral right to take wealth from those who have produced it in order to make up for its failure to collect the economic rent of land which, whether we like it or not, has been created by society working and playing in concert, all we do is further to perpetuate the confusion that results from bad premises and fouled-up logic.

To put the same thought in another way, our trouble lies in our time-honored custom of allowing landowners to appropriate most of the socially created values, instead of insisting that they be used to pay for the services of government. Landowners, having taken for themselves the rent for land, which rent should have been used for public revenue, and then having, by that very process, reduced the wages of those who produced the wealth, have influenced the government to levy taxes, based almost entirely on production, in order to pay for government services which landowners should have paid for in the first place. As it now is, we ask all producers to pay a double tax, one in rent to landowners and one by law to legally constituted tax authorities. All this occurs because we do not respect the rights of ownership of those who produce the wealth and because we do not claim the land as the common heritage of all.

5

Go into any college bookstore and examine the books dealing with aspects of political economy. The evidence will convince you that there are presumed to be only two kinds of economic procedures, namely such as are capitalistic or communistic. We strongly suspect that few books dealing with the taxation of land values will be found. This means that most professors are not using such material. To most people this fact is enough to persuade them that there must be some good reason for this generally accepted attitude. But such a conclusion is not justified. A veritable blanket of wool has been pulled over the eyes of most of the John Does in America. A growing number of college professors are coming to realize the seriousness of this situation.

We implore our modern universities to study ways of developing a far better brand of economy than that of modern modified capitalism or of out-and-out communism—an economy that would be the result of a synthesis of the best in capitalism and the best in communism. Capitalism in America, considering the phenomenal growth and development in this country, cannot be all bad, despite the fact that what made American capitalism seemingly so effective was its access to millions of square miles of fertile and mineral-laden, but unimproved, land. Neither can communism in Russia and China be all bad. A recent visitor to China, one who had been born and raised there came back to say that there is no doubt that communism has greatly benefited the common people of China. Whereas, in his day, the poor, landless Chinese lived wretched and poverty stricken lives, they are now well fed, comfortably, if not aesthetically, clothed and, after a fashion, housed. The change in security status is unmistakable. He did seem to sense that some of the spontaniety of the Chinese people that he once knew had suffered in the process. He remembered them as a fun-loving and humor-filled people, but they seemed to have lost some of the sheer joy of living.

The very frenzy of spirit manifested by those who defend each system is evidence that there are some good things about our modified capitalism and even about communism. Can we not become selective in our thinking and separate the good from the bad, to create a synthesis which would serve the best interests of all citizens and guarantee that the glamour and excitement of living need not erode? Naturally, the super-rich of capitalism and the power cliques of communism will resist such an amalgam of the best of two worlds. Since they are "on top" and in charge, they are all well satisfied. It is they who control the media which alone might create a new public opinion.

There is little doubt that such an idea could gain momentum only in a democratic environment where there is at least a modicum of free expression. The burden of bringing off such a synthesis would rest entirely with us. First, we would have to demonstrate its effectiveness by putting its principles to work. This is, in itself, an almost impossible dream, but it is surprising what happens to an idea when its time has come. Certainly, the need is now. Whether the need can be translated into action, in view of the almost universal ignorance of the principles involved, depends upon whether enough effective leadership can be generated to spread the word and bring about a change in public understanding.

## 6

When one is compelled to list the good things about communism his troubles multiply. The fact is that there is all too little in it that is "good." It does effectively deal with the maldistribution of wealth, something that LVTaxation, even if complete and total, cannot do suddenly and all at once. In one fell swoop, a communist takeover denies the perquisites of ownership to all who might formerly have owned and controlled most of the land and most of the wealth that labor has produced.

In many countries where a take-over by the communists has become a real threat the landowners (always working behind the scene) will engineer a military take-over and see that the state is placed under martial law. This will give the state the power to tighten the screws and make any outspoken criticism of the regime a criminal offense. This has been the almost routine procedure in Latin and South America. This sets the stage for a fascist dictatorship. In case the takeover is communist inspired the law of rent will no longer be predictable. Should the new ruling clique be composed of rough, adventurous war lords whose intention is to supplant the former owners and to appropriate their rent-take, with no intention of relieving or improving the conditions of labor, the law of rent will still function. But in a communist regime the law will be disregarded and in its place an authorized group of men will attempt to steer the economy. Everything now will depend upon the character and wisdom of the new leadership. Natural pressures will still be at work but the law of rent will not be entirely valid, because those underlying regulatory features in a wholly competitive society will no longer be in control. These must give way to deliberate human decisions. No longer is there a basic underlying process to provide a regulatory influence. The conscious decisions of the Politburo will at least partially determine the flow of wealth, although the natural pressures of the law of rent will still be evident.

Such a sudden wresting of wealth from the aristocracy, and the assumption of power to redistribute the wealth by fiat, does have some healing results. Unfortunately, the shifting of authority to another group of human beings will not guarantee that such authority will be exercised wisely; for a time, perhaps yes, but in the long run, probably not. Anyway, in the early stages of a communist takeover, the very power of the Politburo to redistribute both land and wealth may have an enormously good effect upon the welfare of the masses. What happens as the landowners are liquidated is quite another matter! However, the immediate needs of the masses are met and hunger and misery, long suffered, are allayed. One has a hard time finding much else in the system that is good, except the sudden and total redistribution of wealth. Obviously, this process has not taken into account the importance of allowing the individual to possess what he produces. The state arbitrarily appropriates all wealth produced and presumably uses it for the benefit of all.

# 7

For centuries the church has overemphasized the virtues of charity and cautiously underemphasized the basic requirements of justice. Religious traditions were set long before anyone had experienced life under democratic forms of government. Because the need for charity was so glaringly obvious, it was natural that those who were spiritually sensitive would think in those terms. The pity always is that when deprivation and human suffering become widespread and intense there are a steadily diminishing few who react sympathetically. Where greed has had its way with the system most people shrug their shoulders and say, "That's the way it is," and refuse to share their own good fortune. The ways of injustice have so firmly fixed themselves upon human beings everywhere that ultimately only a sensitive minority of the super-affluent are inclined to respond to the appeals to extend charity to the economically depressed. There is little doubt but that charity will always have its place in this world, but economic charity should translate itself into economic intelligence. It is true that it is more blessed to give than to receive, but it is *far more blessed to be able to give than to have to receive*. In a properly ordered world, all except those who are physically or mentally handicapped would be able to take care of themselves and everyone would be expected to do so.

Some years ago a distinguished writer visited Swarthmore College, a Quaker-oriented institution. It is not customary to invite a guest speaker to address the Quaker Meeting but it was rumored that a famous authoress would be present and it was assumed that the Spirit might prompt her to make a few remarks. She came, and the congregation awaited her contribution in anticipation. Time passed as others deferred, and they waited. At last she arose, and drawing herself up to her full height, she said, "The Earth is the Lord's," and sat down. A pause ensued. At last the silence was broken as a professor of philosophy arose and said, "If the earth is the Lord's he is having a lot of trouble with his title." We might ruefully add that the Lord has been having trouble with his title for centuries and that this is probably the cause of most of his disappointments with his most cherished creation, and also the reason why he was obliged to drive man out of the mythical garden of bounty and beauty. Oh, I am quite aware that there are other sins than "gouging the poor" by raising their rents, but if I were inclined to indulge in religious fantasy, knowing what I do, I could be persuaded to accept the idea that claiming the rights to all the perquisites involved in the private ownership of land was the "apple" that got man into trouble from the very start.

CHAPTER ELEVEN

# Where Can We Go From Here?

It would certainly be inappropriate if, having written a book on the need for LVTaxation, we would neglect to indicate what should be done, and how to go about laying the foundation for a better real estate tax policy in the nation. Hedged in as we are by custom, stymied by constitutional requirements and legal terminology, and confronted with an almost total lack of understanding, not only on the part of the public but on the part of those whose business it is to oversee the property tax procedures in states, counties and local communities, prospects for quick success are very slight. However, there are some things that can be done by tax authorities without any recourse to change in the law. There are many others in positions of responsibility who might exert enormous influence, now that it is becoming increasingly clear that we simply cannot continue to operate in conventional ways.

According to the constitution, Congress has the power to levy taxes, not only income taxes (a relatively recent form of taxation), but all kinds of taxes. Traditionally, by employing the principle of subsidiarity, the Federal Government has authorized the various states to initiate and supervise the property tax, and the states, have, by the same principle, authorized cities and counties to assess property and to collect taxes according to basic procedures established by state law. However, every state has its own method of approaching the problem and the legal terminology employed by each state reveals a wide variety, even in the understanding of what kinds of property are taxable. In some states, before LVTaxation could be instituted, a constitutional amendment would have to be voted on by the people.

Under the circumstances the quickest and best way to deal with the problem is for the Federal Government to provide intelligent directives by laying down guide lines for the various states to follow in determining how real estate should be taxed. This could be done without abrogating the right and power of the states to collect and dispense funds raised by the property tax.

Should the Federal Government decree that assessors in all states assess all land at full market value, and instead of using the selling price of land as the tax base, to make as accurate an estimate of the annual rental value of land as possible, using that figure upon which to base the tax, it would in no way take away the right of the state to collect and dispense tax funds.

This basic principle, namely the assessment of all land, either vacant or improved, at full market value, would provide a giant step toward economic revitalization. The effects would be suprising enough even though it would represent only a fraction of what would constitute total LVTaxation. If, in passing such a law, the Federal Government would establish special schools in various sections of the country where the fine points of assessing property, and especially the most precise methods of determining how to arrive at the annual rental value of all kinds of land could be taught, another giant step would have been taken.

Frankly, the widespread lack of understanding on this issue would preclude the likelihood that any directives might be forthcoming from the Federal Government. Action on state levels is not entirely out of the question, but local officials who might be convinced that a land value tax would be a stimulus to business need not wait for any special legislation. In most states assessors are instructed to assess land at full market value. Very few ever do, but that is already the basic law in many states. If tax officials would simply follow the law to the letter as far as the land is concerned, and value buildings as low as possible, surprising results would follow.

Judge James Clarkson, the ex-mayor of Southfield, Michigan, a suburb immediately adjacent to Detroit, believed in LVTaxation but there was no law permitting the exclusive taxation of land value in that state (or any state, for that matter). However there were vast acreages in Southfield that were vacant and these had been ridiculously underassessed for years. Without doing anything contrary to the basic law, he ordered all such land to be assessed at full market value. Considering the fact that land in Southfield was ripe for development and was being priced at fabulous heights, the sudden changes in assessments caused great consternation among the landowners. They sued, but always lost their cases because the Mayor was actually doing what the law said should be done. Previous assessors had listened to the landowners who happily had watched their properties appreciate rapidly as new highways in the area were completed. With higher assessments the vacant land brought substantially lower prices and several large firms bought land and erected fine buildings to serve as headquarters. The contrast between what was happening in Southfield and what was going on in Detroit was obvious at a glance, especially along one street where one side was in Detroit and the other in Southfield.

Not every community would find a proper assessment of land as effective, but the very first step toward a proper assessment roll in any community is the accurate evaluation of the annual rental value of land. In order to do this an assessor should be an expert in determining the value of the buildings that might be on the land. Any assessor is in a key position, and if he does his work with skill and understanding he can enormously effect the quality of life in his community. For this reason all assessors should be career men and trained in special schools, the same as doctors, lawyers, ministers, teachers, nurses, pharmacists and the various kinds of engineers. They might then enjoy as much prestige as mayors, commissioners or comptrollers.

Partial land value taxation is now legal in Pennsylvania. A law, known as the Graded Tax Law,* gives all city councils of the forty-eight cities of the third class the authority to transfer any or all of the city taxes from the combined value of land and buildings to land value exclusively. We say "partial" because the city tax represents between twenty and thirty per cent of the entire property tax. School and county taxes are levied in the conventional manner.

It was in 1960 that I agreed to represent the Economic Education League of Albany, New York in a number of cities in Western Pennsylvania. Everywhere I went I ran into an abysmal lack of understanding about real estate taxes. Rotary and Kiwanis Clubs, Chambers of Commerce and Womens' Clubs all believe in free speech. That is, they will gladly listen to almost anything as long as it is free. A retired professor of economics, Dr. Harry G. Brown, and I visited about fifteen cities. We talked and interviewed and explained, hoping that some citizens might step forward to take up the cudgels for land value taxation. There were always a few who reacted favorably, but for the most part, it was hard to convince many that real estate taxes were all that important.

In Erie, I taught a class made up of ten members of the Junior Chamber of Commerce. They got the message and we organized ELTA, the Erie Land Tax Association. Despite the fact that ELTA had in its membership a number of outstanding leaders in many walks of life, such as realtors, lawyers, manufacturers, insurance men, salesmen, bankers and many others, it was impossible to reconstruct the thinking of enough people or to enlist the efforts of those who "just didn't understand."

Erie City Council was urged to adopt LVTaxation. Did they? They did not, for the simple reason that so many people in town, and one far too powerful landowner in particular, had hang-up trouble. They could not conceive of the fact that it was tax trouble that had the city stuck on dead center, or that a tax on land value could be any different in its effects than a tax based on land and buildings together. They had been conditioned to believe that decay and obsolescence were normal, that slums were inevitable, that somehow, if anything was done, the Federal Government would have to do it. They knew it would take $10,000 to buy a choice lot and that the tax on a fine home would be exorbitant; but no one had ever explained why these things were so. They were hung-up on the idea that it would be a mistake to give industries a break, as if industries had nothing to do with providing jobs. They had no idea what wonderful things might happen to the entire city if the owner of a vacant lot, assessed at $1,000 was obliged to pay a city tax of $70.00 instead of the conventional escape tax of $10.00.

* Act No. 299, August 1951. Amended as per Senate Bill 535, April 1959.

There they were, thoroughly conditioned to live under a tax system that was designed to make land expensive and to add multiple taxes to everything they had to buy, so that, by the time they bought whatever they needed, the cumulative costs would be killing everybody. All the time the wheels of misfortune would keep turning, gradually squeezing the very life out of the economy. But any implication that a city might come alive, should land value taxation be adopted, was just too much. Although there is a growing interest across America in the principles of land value taxation, and dedicated Georgists are active in many cities and states, time is running out and public awareness must be developed as rapidly as possible.

Ruefully, we recall the colossal policy blunders that were the hallmark of the sixties. Because it was assumed that our show of military power had been responsible for stemming the tides of communism in Western Europe, and seeing the growing threat of communist expansion in East Asia, the policy makers of America—with very little opposition from either church or university leadership—sold the American people on the idea that we could stem the tides of revolution in the Orient by meeting ideas with force. The whole venture was a fiasco and fifty thousand young men were sacrificed, along with billions of dollars spent and precious resources destroyed. Rather than using force we might well have stopped communism dead in its tracks if we had been prepared to use ideas instead of standing armies and the fear of dreadful reprisals. As it now stands we could be victims of another military disaster, whether we win or lose, because we are still not prepared to show the rest of the world how to resolve its economic and social problems.

Then, there was that totally inept but appealing idea that we could wipe out poverty by drawing upon tax funds and appropriating billions of dollars to assist the poor in reordering their lives. Certainly, most of those who helped get the movement underway knew it would never work. A few years later, after spending 12½ billions on the poverty program and many billions more on welfare and urban renewal projects we have more poverty than ever before.

But still another colossal folly awaits an ignominious demise. The idea that we can renew the obsolescence and decay that has overtaken the cities of America by using tax funds, raised under policies that had brought the decay on in the first place, buying run-down sections of central city areas, erecting fine buildings and relocating those businesses that were strong enough to pay the "discounted" bills involved. Having done nothing to correct the trends toward obsolescence, we blunder on to discover that vast areas—hundreds of acres or dozens of square miles—have become an urban wasteland, destined to be abandoned by city dwellers and eventually to become the responsibility of the city because the owners will no longer pay their taxes.

Superficial critics of what has been known as "The Single Tax" have often scoffed because those who advocate it see it as a sort of patent social medicine that will cure all of our economic woes. We do not see it in such an extravagant light but we are prepared to say that most of the indicators point to answers and solutions to problems that have been baffling the uninitiated for years. At a meeting of some members of a Chamber of Commerce in a certain Pennsylvania city, one individual proceeded to enumerate a number of projects in which they were then engaged, and remarked "If we would just press for the adoption of land value taxation all of these issues would be easily resolved."

Our world is desperately in need of a more equitable distribution of the wealth that is being or could be produced in every land. As we see it, America is in a beautiful position to demonstrate how it can be done. Most of the madness that we are experiencing is caused by "gross inequity" and that, in turn, is caused by private collection of rent. This can be changed only by a correct tax policy and this can be done only when a wide understanding of the principles involved has been developed.

Without realizing what we were doing, by taxing land and buildings alike, we instituted injustice and greed. We could just as easily, had we only known, have instituted justice and goodwill. We have done it many times and we can do it again. Our founding fathers did just that when they incorporated the Bill of Rights into the Constitution. Evils, long endured, were declared illegal. When they guaranteed us freedom of religion, freedom of speech and freedom of assembly they instituted tolerance and goodwill. When they separated church and state they instituted intelligent forebearance. Now the time has come to add to the decrees which govern the affairs of our people by instituting a new tax policy which will usher in a new day of economic justice, and which could demonstrate to the rest of the world how men can achieve a high degree of equity. Only thus can we ever hope to deal with the tensions which are threatening to overwhelm us.

And so, we sign off. Yours for beautiful cities where slums are no more, where everyone (not all except from four to ten per cent ) are happily engaged in some useful occupation, enjoying a high level of security and well being, freed from the tortuous feeling that no one wants them and confident that dreams and aspirations can become the realities of their tomorrows.

## INCENTIVE TAXATION FOR YORK, PENNSYLVANIA (IT)

A Research Study by Wylie Young
Author of
"Antidote for Madness"

York, one of forty-eight cities of the Third Class in Pennsylvania, has been granted the right to base all or part of the city tax on land value, rather than upon the combined value of land and buildings. This was done at the recommendation of the Pittsburgh Chamber of Commerce and the Real Estate Board of that city.

Very few people knew what was involved. Our schools, reacting to the pressures of entrenched interests, failed to teach that a tax based upon land value could not be passed on to the user or buyer of the land, and it also failed to teach that all taxes based upon labor products are always passed on and must be paid by the ultimate user, whether he be the landowner or the renter. These basic economic laws have been completely overlooked. The almost universal failure on the part of people to realize the significance of these facts has made it extremely difficult to convince city council members that to do this would vastly improve the economy of their city.

### THE KEY TO PROPER TAXATION

Almost all tax policies now in vogue are the exact opposite of what they should be. Most of our taxes are based upon labor products (buildings and improvements attached to land), labor itself (income taxes) or on the right to trade (sales). These are all punitive and they all tend to discourage or prevent the production of wealth. We have, without knowing it, developed a tax system that makes it hard for people to produce, or to own or enjoy the wealth they do produce.

It is not necessary to tax labor products. If we had the wit to base all taxes on land value we would discover that land would become available at lower prices and everything from needles to skyscrapers would be cheaper. It is because we tax land value so lightly that land prices are so high, and the high cost of land is what keeps the brakes so tightly set on all kinds of business activity.

The reason that taxes on land value are not passed on is that the quantity of land is fixed. No one can produce more. No one can move a landsite from one place to another. Its value, whether because of fertility, location or undersoil deposits, is determined by the willingness of people to bid for the right to use it.

Labor products fall under a different set of influences. If more of anything is desired, more can be produced. Buildings can be constructed, remodeled, destroyed and sometimes even moved. There is no fixed limit to the number or quality of things that can be produced.

### OUR MISEDUCATED GENERATION

Very few people understand these basic facts. They are seldom ever mentioned in high schools or colleges. Most well informed people resent any implication that our educational institutions are to blame. Many who do understand think they know why so many generations of students have been short-changed. The fact remains that if the full economic rent of land were to be collected by the state in lieu of taxes on labor products the buying or selling price of land would be reduced to zero, and that this, coupled with the exemption of all buildings and improvements, would cause living costs to plummet phenomenally. The very idea that land prices would be reduced to zero sounds, to people who have been conditioned by our educational institutions, as crazy nonsense. The prevailing lie that progress is always associated with rising land prices is deeply embedded in our social consciousness. Actually those rising land prices are the forerunners of increased rents and lower wage rates for all who work or render worthwhile service.

Such comments are received by most people — all products of our educational system—with shocked incredulity. "If this is true" they say, "and if our failure to tax land at its real value and our insistence upon taxing buildings is so bad, why has our ignorance not been disastrous?" Our reply is, "It has been monstrously disastrous, but very few understand why we are being plagued with so many social and economic problems."

Overlooking a whole flood of negative effects we are now involved in a life and death struggle with inflation, not realizing that high land prices and exorbitant building costs are only symptoms of the artificially generated inflation of land prices which is really at the bottom of the outrageous prices being asked for old houses on artificially scarce land, not to mention the out-of-sight cost of everything we need for comforts and conveniences.

## BACK TO THE GRASS ROOTS

To say that by taxing land value and untaxing buildings we could usher in a new day strikes most people as sheer nonsense, Very few even try to understand. They just walk away. Because there is a law in Pennsylvania that gives 48 cities of the third class the right to shift city taxes from buildings to land value all mayors and councilmen of these cities are receiving a publication called "Incentive Taxation." They know about the law but do not always know how it might be applied in their city. Harrisburg has started to use the law and other cities are seriously considering it.

Sixty years ago Pittsburgh was granted the right to begin taxing land value higher and building values lower. Immediately, the land being held by speculators on the outskirts of the city came into use. Those people who make it their business to take advantage of the low tax on land which enables them to hold land out of use until some hard working individual or firm is willing to pay a high price for the land, will see the hand-writing on the wall and will get rid of the land. Buyers will, cannily enough, not pay them as much as they had hoped to get, but the pressure will be on and the land will come into use. With the prospect of not having to pay such high taxes on the proposed buildings the buyers will be inclined to build bigger and better buildings.

Pittsburgh has greatly benefited by its having been allowed to levy higher taxes on land than on buildings. Many of those fine buildings in the Golden Triangle save from $15,000 to $30,000 in taxes each year. The Alcoa building saves over $30,000. The erstwhile headquarters of the U. S. Steel Company has saved $60,000 annually. The new U. S. Steel Building saves upwards of $100,000 annually. This passed New Year Eve the City Council voted to raise the millage on land value from 49.5 to 97.5 mills during 1979. This was done instead of raising the wage tax, thus saving the working homeowners a considerable amount of money. Naturally, this did not please those who owned rented properties Their reaction was quite vocal but even large landowners will discover that the change will benefit them in other ways.

## PROPERTY TAX FIGURES IN YORK

Before we can enter into an intelligent discussion of incentive taxation we must first note how the present property tax in York is instituted. As every property owner should know, all three of the local taxing authorities (county, city and school board) base the tax on the combined assessments of land and buildings, as follows:

| | |
|---|---|
| Total land assessments | $24,194,940 |
| Total building assessments | 118,309,555 |
| Grand total | 142,504,495 |

Millage rates are: County - 4 mls; City - 20.4 mls; School - 36 mls.

By dividing building assessments by land assessments (118,309,555 divided by 24,194,940) we find that property owners in York are paying 4.89 times as much on buildings as on land. This is certainly not right but it is fairly normal in Pennsylvania cities. For purposes of discussion we may as well say it is five times as much. Amounts collected by each authority are as follows:

| | | | | | |
|---|---|---|---|---|---|
| County tax on bldgs. | $473,238 | – on land | $96,779 | Total tax | $570,017 |
| City tax on bldgs. | 2,413,514 | - " " | 493,576 | " " | 2,907,090 |
| School tax on bldgs. | 4,259,143 | - " " | 871,017 | " " | 8,607,267 |

At this point we must keep in mind that the York City Council is the only tax authority authorized to shift either part or all of the city tax from buildings to land value. No referendum is required. The city is currently collecting $2,907,090. The first requirement would be to determine how many mills would be needed to raise the same amount of money from land assessments alone. Total land assessments being $2,903,392 we find that 120.2 mills will bring $2,908,231. In computing the incentive tax on any individual property all we need do is multiply the land assessment by .1202. Naturally we would then compare it with the present tax. In some instances the tax would be exactly the same. In some cases it would be more and in some less.

## THE GRADUAL APPROACH

Our suggestion is that we embark upon a program of increasing the millage on land value and decreasing the millage on buildings with each successive year for four years. Beginning with 1980 we can begin by

Note: Before becoming involved with the figures on the next two pages, we suggest that the reader turn to page 112 and finish the main text. A few aspects of the figure chart will be unclear unless this is done.

On this page: the present system of basing the tax on land and buildings. showing (1) assessments; (2) ratio between land and bldgs. (3) tax now.

First, check a few homes. 9 out of 10 will pay lower taxes, a few will pay more if

| Property | Land Asmt. | Bldg. Asmt. | Total Asmt. | Ratio | Tax Now |
|---|---|---|---|---|---|
| 35 S. Penn. | $420 | $2,520 | $2,940 | 1 to 6 | $59.97 |
| 37 S. Penn. | 420 | 3,085 | 3,605 | 1 to 7.3 | 73.54 |
| 46 Newbury | 420 | 2,030 | 2,450 | 1 to 4.8 | 49.98 |
| 56 Newbury | 350 | 3,295 | 3,710 | 1 to 9.4 | 75.68 |
| 167 Irving | 2,700 | 19,565 | 22,365 | 1 to 7.2 | 456.00 |
| 30 -32 E. College | 1,260 | 11,655 | 12,915 | 1 to 9.2 | 263.00 |
| 909 McKenzie | 2,240 | 14,490 | 16,730 | 1 to 6.5 | 341.00 |
| 900 S. George | 8,190 | 40,005 | 48,195 | 1 to 4.9 | 982.00 |
| 543 W. King | 1,050 | 10,710 | 11,760 | 1 to 10 | 239.00 |

Industries are "do-ers"—They operate on relatively low value land and invest heavily

| Property | Land Asmt. | Bldg. Asmt. | Total Asmt. | Ratio | Tax Now |
|---|---|---|---|---|---|
| Orinake Mills | 22.575 | 253,505 | 276,080 | 1 to 11 | $5,632 |
| York Hoover Co. | 6,895 | 64,995 | 71,890 | 1 to 9.5 | 1,466 |
| Carnation Co. | 19,845 | 212,660 | 232,505 | 1 to 11 | 4,743 |
| Koppers Co. | 47,810 | 418,740 | 466,550 | 1 to 8.7 | 9,517 |
| Norad Hosery | 38,535 | 942,655 | 981,190 | 1 to 24 | 20,001 |
| Sunshine Investment | 3,500 | 62,685 | 66,185 | 1 to 18 | 1,350 |
| York Wall Paper | 16,100 | 138,600 | 154,700 | 1 to 8.6 | 1,935 |
| Danskin | 29,365 | 915,705 | 945,070 | 1 to 31 | 19,279 |

High taxes on buildings in center-city discourages construction of appropriate buildings.

| Property | Land Asmt. | Bldg. Asmt. | Total Asmt. | Ratio | Tax Now |
|---|---|---|---|---|---|
| Steller - 515 S. Geo. | 6,650 | 59,850 | 66,500 | 1 to 9 | 1,356 |
| P.A.& S Small Co. | 11,095 | 121,135 | 132,230 | 1 to 11 | 2,697 |
| White Rose 237 S. Ct. | 2,100 | 20,300 | 22,400 | 1 to 9.6 | 456 |
| York Federal | 33,355 | 195,860 | 229,210 | 1 to 5.8 | 4,675 |
| Nat. Bank & Trust | 111,230 | 631,680 | 742,910 | 1 to 5.8 | 15,155 |
| 700-710 E. Market | 17,605 | 100,100 | 117,705 | 1 to 5.6 | 2,401 |
| 622-650 W. Poplar | 11,060 | 53,515 | 64,575 | 1 to 4.8 | 1,317 |
| White Rose E. Markt. | 20, 055 | 113,050 | 133,105 | 1 to 5.6 | 2,715 |

Far too many businesses in York are obliged to operate in obsolete buildings.

| Property | Land Asmt. | Bldg. Asmt. | Total Asmt. | Ratio | Tax Now |
|---|---|---|---|---|---|
| York Bank & Trust | 53,235 | 6,615 | 59,850 | 1 to 0.1 | 1,220 |
| Farmers Fire Ins. | 20,965 | 27,615 | 48,580 | 1.1.3 | 991 |
| 9-11 E. Market | 33,425 | 20,545 | 53.970 | 1 to 0.6 | 1,100 |
| 19-21 E. George | 29,855 | 5,320 | 35,175 | 1 to 0.17 | 717 |
| 45-49 N. George | 66,890 | 32,795 | 99,685 | 1 to 0.49 | 2,033 |
| 53-55 W. Market | 33,320 | 19,219 | 52,539 | 1 to 0.57 | 1,071 |
| 35-47 N. Beaver | 61,145 | 33,040 | 94,105 | 1 to 0.54 | 1,919 |
| Woolworth | 95,830 | 19,380 | 115,210 | 1 to 0.2 | 2,350 |
| 54 W. Market | 50,120 | 22,120 | 72,240 | 1 to 0.44 | 1,473 |

The tax system should encourage people to put land to its highest and best use.

| Property | Land Asmt. | Bldg. Asmt. | Total Asmt. | Ratio | Tax Now |
|---|---|---|---|---|---|
| 46 E. Phila. St. | 3,220 | 5,250 | 8,470 | 1 to 1.6 | 172 |
| 50 E. Phila. St. | 2,205 | 4,025 | 6,230 | 1 to 1.8 | 127 |

The central city should be used for commerce and trade. It should be a concentrated area for conferring and dealing. On the perimeter of the downtown area fine luxury apartments should house many who could walk to their work. Fine department stores and well appointed malls, multi-storied office buildings

LOOKING TO THE ADOPTION OF INCENTIVE TAXATION (IT)

**On this page: showing how taxes on particular properties will be either higher or lower, depending on the ratio of land value to building value.**

**the houses are obsolete or located on large lots or high priced land.**

| 15 mills on B.—46 on L | 10 on B—71.3 on L | 5 on B—95 on L | 120.2 on L |
|---|---|---|---|
| $55.91 | $53.29 | $52.00 | $50.48 |
| 57.49 | 55.14 | 52.50 | 50.48 |
| 50.14 | 50.24 | 50.05 | 50.48 |
| 65.83 | 57.90 | 49.72 | 42.00 |
| 420 | 387 | 354 | 324 |
| 234 | 205 | 178 | 151 |
| 322 | 304 | 285 | 269 |
| 983 | 983 | 778 | 982 |
| 210 | 182 | 153 | 126 |

**in plant facilities. They provide jobs and do not deserve to be penalized.**

| | | | |
|---|---|---|---|
| 4,860 | 4,144 | 3,411 | 2,713 |
| 1,297 | 1,141 | 979 | 828 |
| 4.119 | 3,540 | 2,948 | 2,385 |
| 8,489 | 7,595 | 6,634 | 5,746 |
| 15,976 | 12,173 | 8,373 | 4,631 |
| 1,104 | 875 | 645 | 420 |
| 2,834 | 2,533 | 3,222 | 1,935 |
| 15,122 | 11,250 | 7,367 | 3,529 |

**By lowering taxes on buildings construction of all kinds will be encouraged.**

| | | | |
|---|---|---|---|
| 1,209 | 1,073 | 931 | 799 |
| 2,337 | 1 805 | 1,659 | 1,333 |
| 402 | 352 | 300 | 252 |
| 4,501 | 4,336 | 4,147 | 4,009 |
| 14,691 | 14,246 | 13,724 | 13,368 |
| 2,326 | 2,256 | 2,172 | 2,116 |
| 1,320 | 1,323 | 1,317 | 1,329 |
| 2,635 | 2,559 | 2,470 | 2,410 |

**Landowners cannot afford high building costs plus high taxes on new buildings.**

| | | | |
|---|---|---|---|
| 2,595 | 3,861 | 5,090 | 6,398 |
| 1,397 | 1,770 | 2,129 | 2,519 |
| 1,875 | 2,588 | 3,277 | 4,017 |
| 1,479 | 2,207 | 2,862 | 3,588 |
| 3,628 | 5,260 | 6,517 | 8,040 |
| 1,850 | 2,567 | 3,261 | 4,005 |
| 3,362 | 4,689 | 5,973 | 7,349 |
| 4,784 | 7,025 | 9,199 | 11,518 |
| 2.681 | 3,794 | 4,871 | 6,024 |

**Single dwelling houses or heavy industries do not belong in center city areas.**

| | | | |
|---|---|---|---|
| 229 | 281 | 331 | 387 |
| 163 | 197 | 229 | 265 |

**and hotels, government buildings and parking ramps should be located in the central business district. Colleges, schools and churches only tend to get in the way. Inasmuch as they are tax-exempt anyway they should be put where the people are working—not living.**

levying 15 mills on buildings and 46.9 mills on land value. In 1981 a 10 mill levy on buildings would call for a 71.3 mill levy on land. In 1982 a five mill levy on buildings would require a 95 mill levy on land. By 1983 we could eliminate any tax based on buildings and by using 120.2 mills raise all revenue on land value alone. Each year the same amount of revenue would be raised by taxing land value as by taxing land and buildings alike.

## LET THE FIGURES TELL THE STORY

In most cities there are three types of properties— residential, industrial and commercial. In the figure chart we present figures showing present assessments and present taxes on a few of each such types of properties. In additional columns we show what the tax would be if the millage rate on land was increased and the building rate was decreased so much each year, until by the fourth year the entire tax was based on land value only. A quick glance at the column marked "ratio" will enable the reader to see instantly whether the "IT" tax will be more or less than before. In the city as a whole property owners pay 4.89 times as much on buildings as on land. Therefore, when the "IT" tax is instituted any particular property will require either a higher or lower tax depending on the ratio of land to building assessment. If the ratio happens to be 1 to 4.89 (the average ratio in the city) the tax will be exactly the same. If the ratio is 1 to more than 4.89 the tax will be lower. If the ratio is 1 to less than 4.89 the tax will be relatively higher.

## RATIOS FAVOR HOMEOWNERS AND INDUSTRIES

Approximately 90% of the homeowners in any city will enjoy lower taxes under the incentive tax, The land values are relatively low and people do put their hearts and souls into their homes. Sometimes ratios will be 1 to 8, 10, or 15. Example: Total assessments on 11 homes from 603 to 643 on Pershing are: on land, $8,785; on buildings, $69,340. (B ÷ L = 7.89) or a fraction less than 8. With the average ratio being 1 to 8 the taxes on all but one home would be lower. That one showed a ratio of 1 to 4.40. If a residence, as some are in York, is located on central-city high-value land the ratio might be as bad as 1 to .9. Most of such buildings are being rented and many such properties in older cities are owned by absentee landowners. After all, one family houses do do not belong in center-city. Under incentive taxation fine luxury apartments do belong.

Industries almost invariably will enjoy reduced taxes. They should. After-all, industries provide jobs and greatly add to the economy of a city. Under our present system thay pay first, a high price for land, and second, an exorbitant penalty tax. Traditionally they just shrug it off and pass the tax on in the price of their product. The competition does the same, so they say to themselves, "What's the difference." Meanwhile city officials, accustomed to taxing buildings, rub their hands in glee when a manufacturing company adds an expensive new building to their plant.

## LOSERS TODAY BUT BIG WINNERS TOMORROW

Commercial properties, especially those in central city areas, all too often show ratios where land values are high and building values low. The reason: The prospective tax on any building appropriate to the area is so great that landowners elect to rent old buildings to struggling merchants at high rents. The tax on any new building would eliminate any possible profit that might be derived by investing in a good building. The only viable solution is for the taxing authorities to tax land value high, keeping the price of land low, and to exempt all buildings, so that fine structures can be built. Thus, the landowners would make their money not by taking unfair advantage of people, but by investing in capital goods, and so increasing the supply of real wealth and enriching the lives of those who actually produce and distribute the wealth.

We need not allow our sympathy for those whose taxes will be raised to deter our enthusiasm. In the long run they will benefit as much as anyone. We should bear in mind that homeowners and manufacturing firms have been paying far more than they should. Besides, they have invested heavily in buildings and have contributed to the enhancement of all land values — theirs and adjacent properties as well. For this they do not deserve to be punished every year.

## WOULD IT BE WORTH ALL THE TROUBLE?

Naturally, those who find this system new and different will be asking if a change to the (IT) system is worth all the trouble. Our contention is that, as now instituted, the property tax is a mere indiscriminate way of raising public revenue. It should be transformed into a system that guarantees justice and fair play to all, and at the same time puts a stop to the automatic grants of special privilege to those who choose to use their landownership as a means of exploitation.

For those cities of the Third Class in Pennsylvania who do not operate under a Home Rule Charter the prospect for change is limited. They are obliged to apply the incentive tax to city taxes only. Some six or seven third class cities do operate under the Home Rule Charter and these are permitted to extend the application of the principle to other taxing authorities. Although Pittsburgh has enjoyed a small amount of land value taxation for over fifty years, recently a Home Rule Charter was adopted and that is the reason that the city council voted to make up a deficit in the budget by increasing the tax on land value from 47.5 mills to 97.5 .

## ASSESSMENT PRACTICES MUST BE CHANGED

When a legislative body assumes that land and buildings are alike it will make no allowance for the fact that taxes based on land will produce entirely different effects than taxes based on buildings. Knowing that it is wrong to tax buildings we understand that it is disastrous to assess buildings at full market value. The proper way to assess is to forget the building value entirely, except as its presence tends to enhance or diminish the value of the adjoining land. Moreover, the idea of assessing land at a percentage of its appraised value only tends to emasculate the proper objective of holding the price of land down. Of course those who regard land speculation as a morally legitimate way of making money will disagree. This does not alter the fact that literally trillions of dollars have lined the pockets of "do nothing land speculators" and caused millions of people no end of trouble.

Only by assessing land at its full market value and doing this with all land holdings can true equity or parity be established. To talk about the necessity of being fair to all property owners and at the same time to tax land and buildings alike is to be guilty of both illogical and fallacious thinking. It has been going on for years and really is at the bottom of most of our economic woes. In those countries where land is exempt and buildings and improvements are obliged to carry the tax load, there you will find the worst of all economic and social conditions.

Because of the strategic advantage which landownership conveys there is always a painful period of stress toward the final stages of an economic cycle. Business failures increase and individuals find themselves being squeezed as rents increase and land prices begin to soar. Many will find that they have overreached themselves and will begin to retrench. Time is always on the side of the landowners and they will press their advantage by upping rents and making exorbitant demands on those who might still be able to buy land. We are seeing an almost unbelievable increase in land prices and in the purchase price of old houses that are located in desirable areas. The energy crunch has aggravated the situation as more and more young marrieds find it necessary to buy properties near their work. Wage and salary rates are much higher than they were and the increase is being squeezed away by the outrageous dedemands of landowners. It was ever thus. If you own the land and times get rough you can kick and stab your neighbor when he is down and no one will accuse you of being a cad. That is your constitutional right.

There is only one way to deal with this inhuman process. It is called incentive taxation. It is very difficult to get people to face up to this situation. The average man in the street has a gut feeling that to own land is the magic key to permanent prosperity. Everyone wants to be the squeezer and not the squeezee.

## SELECTED READINGS ON SITE VALUE TAXATION AND RELATED ISSUES


Andelson, Robert V., Editor, Critics of Henry George--A Centenary Appraisal of Their Strictures. Cranbury, N.J.: Associated University Presses, Inc., 1979.

Andelson, Robert V., Imputed Rights--An Essay on Christian Social Theory. Athens: University of Georgia Press, 1971.

Archer, R. W., Site Value Taxation in Central Business Development. Sydney, Australia. Washington: Urban Land Institute, 1972.

Becker, Arthur P., Land and Building Taxes. Madison: University of Wisconsin Press, 1969.

Brandon, Robert M., Jonathan Rowe, and Thomas H. Stanton, Tax Politics: How they make you pay and what you can do about it. New York: Pantheon, 1976.

Brown, Harry Gunnison, Selected Articles by Harry Gunnison Brown--The Case for Land Value Taxation. New York: Robert Schalkenbach Foundation, 1980.

Brown, Harry Gunnison and Elizabeth R. Brown, The Effective Answer to Communism and Why You Don't Get It in College. New York: Robert Schalkenbach Foundation, 1958.

Citizens Housing and Planning Council of New York, How Tax Exemption Broke the Housing Deadlock in New York City. New York: 1960.

Clawson, Marion, Editor, Modernizing Urban Land Policy, Resources for the Future. Baltimore: Johns Hopkins University Press, 1973.

Cord, Steven B., Henry George: Dreamer or Realist? Philadelphia: University of Pennsylvania Press, 1965.

Cord, Steven B., Catalyst! (Selected articles from Incentive Taxation newsletter). New York: Robert Schalkenbach Foundation, 1979.

Douglas, Lord (Christopher Johnson), Land Value Rating, Theory and Practice. London: Garden City Press Ltd., 1961.

Duncan, George H., People, Land and Taxes--A Study of Man's Relationship with Mother Earth and His Fellows. New York: Robert Schalkenbach Foundation, 1954.

Ecker-Race, L. L., The Politics and Economics of State and Local Finance. Englewood Cliffs, N.J.: Prentice Hall, 1970.

Finkelstein, Philip, Real Property Taxation in New York City. New York: Frederick A. Praeger, 1975.

Fuchs, John R., Constructive Taxation for Free Enterprise--A Study of What Is Mine, Thine, and Ours. New York: Exposition Press, 1956.

Geiger, George R., The Philosophy of Henry George (foreword by John Dewey). New York: Macmillan, 1936.

George, Henry, Progress and Poverty. Social Problems. Protection or Free Trade. A Perplexed Philosopher. The Science of Political Economy. The Land Question. New York: Robert Schalkenbach Foundation, 1979, 1981, 1982.

George, Henry, Jr., The Life of Henry George. New York: Robert Schalkenbach Foundation, 1960.

Hapgood, David, The Average Man Fights Back. New York: Doubleday, 1977.

Harriss, C. Lowell, Property Tax Reform: More Progress, Less Poverty. Greencastle, Indiana: De Pauw University, 1970.

Holland, Daniel M., Editor, The Assessment of Land Value. Madison: University of Wisconsin Press, 1970.

Hirsch, Max, Land Value Taxation in Practice: A Record of the Progress in Legislation. West Hartford, Connecticut: John C. Lincoln Institute, 1968.

Newcomb, William W., The Conspiracy against Homeowners and Tenants. Melbourne, Florida: Exposé Books, 1977.

O'Regan, Rolland, Rating in New Zealand. Wainuiomata, New Zealand, 1973.

Rubenstein, Stan, Land and Freedom. New York: Robert Schalkenbach Foundation, 1983.

Tucker, Gilbert M., The Self-Supporting City. New York: Robert Schalkenbach Foundation, 1958

Wallis, Louis, The Bible Is Human--A Study in Secular History. New York: Columbia University Press, 1942.

Williams, Percy, The Pittsburgh Graded Tax Plan. New York: Robert Schalkenbach Foundation, 1964.

# ANTIDOTE FOR MADNESS

*by*

*Wylie Young*

*What every grammar school student should know and understand*
*but*
*which very few of our best educated people*
*either know or understand*

THREE PARAGRAPHS FROM

CHAPTER ONE

# A Cornerstone of Truth

Here then, is an important assertion. You should have it constantly before you as we proceed. Taxes that are based upon anything that has been produced by human labor are *always* passed on to the ultimate consumer. Every economist knows this to be a fact. It is virtually an economic axiom. The inescapable tendency is for such a tax to increase the consumer cost of the item taxed, to limit the quantity that might be produced and eventually to impair its quality. Unfortunately, most of the taxes we pay are based upon labor products, labor itself (incomes) or the right to sell the things we make (sales). This latter is the most outrageous ploy of all.

On the contrary, a tax that is based upon land value *cannot* be passed on, either to the renter or the buyer of land. This assertion is usually made in all economics textbooks, but little or nothing is ever made of it. Yet, here is the crux of our socio-economic problem. Any careful effort to put this well-established fact in its proper perspective would literally revolutionize our life-style. Every economist who is worthy of his salt will admit that a tax on land value cannot be passed on, but too many economists know that there are powerful and influential people who do not want this fact exposed, and so they are certain to get more "salt" if they play the fact down and do not follow through to its ultimate conclusions.

Nevertheless, this is the all-important formula. As the current idiom would have it—"We are laying this proposition on you," that taxes on labor products are *always* passed on, making everything except land more expensive, but taxes based upon land value are *never* passed on, making land cheaper than it otherwise would be. In saying this we are stating one of the most far-reaching and, if it were acted upon intelligently, one of the most revolutionary ideas ever promulgated.

CHAPTER TWO

# Two Entirely Different Entities

In order to appreciate the significance of the two closely related facts, that taxes on land value are never passed on, while taxes on buildings and improvements are always passed on by the landowner to the user or buyer, our first concern must be to point out the reasons why these are facts to be relied upon. Naturally, the one place where both of these facts come into play is in the property tax.

It has become the fashion for speakers or writers to take back-hand slaps at the property tax. Seldom does anyone impart any wisdom on the real issues involved. Never have I heard a single person, either in an important office or running for office, identify the real trouble. One gets the impression that all men in official positions have agreed never to expose the central nerve of the problem, but this suspicion has given way to the doleful realization that "they just don't understand." If someone does venture a recommendation, he usually proves that he does not realize that property taxes involve two entirely different entities, land and buildings. (We should always say "buildings and improvements," but for purposes of brevity we will usually use the one word "buildings" and imply the rest.)

Like Topsy, the property tax in America just grew. In our early days, those who were influential in establishing tax policies never suspected it would make any difference whether they taxed land or buildings, or both together. So we have traditionally levied taxes on both alike, as if they were alike, and as if taxes affected each in identical ways.

Before we can hope to have a meeting of minds, we must distinguish clearly between the nature of land and the nature of whatever improvements may have been made, either by increasing the productive capacity of the land itself or by the construction of buildings. Indeed, unless we can keep land and all types of improvements sharply separated in our thinking, there can be no clarity of thought in the entire field of economics. What then are these differences? It is a fact that land and buildings are as different as chalk and salt, and that taxes affect each in diametrically opposite ways.

## THE NATURE OF LAND

Land is God-made, the given natural resources of our environment. Properly defined, "land is the whole material universe except man and his products." Therefore, land includes forests, lakes, rivers, oceans, the air we breathe and all radio and TV electronic wave-lengths.

## THE NATURE OF BUILDINGS

Buildings are man-made. They are products of human labor and represent a form of wealth. Properly defined, wealth is "any material thing produced by labor from land and having exchange value." A building can be both wealth and capital, depending upon its use.

Now read the column on the right.

---

Land is in limited supply. There is just so much and no more. It can neither be created nor destroyed. No one can manufacture farms, create mines or fabricate a new world. Land is plentiful but not all land is valuable.

Buildings are in limitless supply. If not prevented or if conditions are right we can add any number of buildings we want or need. Buildings are constantly being constructed, repaired, remodeled, replaced or destroyed.

---

Land is the sole source of all wealth, but it is not wealth. We emphasize this because many economics textbooks say that it is so. To do this is to imply that land is a commodity and should be treated as such. This is to commit a grievous error in semantics and leads to hopeless confusion.

A building is wealth, though in many instances it can be both wealth and capital. A house, lived in by its owner is wealth. If it is being rented to residential tenants, or to manufacturers or to store managers it is capital. Any wealth being used to produce more wealth is capital.

---

Land will sometimes increase in value 1000% in a short time. Discovery of some natural deposit or news of a proposed bridge or highway will cause striking increases in value. Such enormous increases are the result of market demand for deposits and/or for the use of advantageous locations.

No building ever increases 1000% in value. Buildings, if destroyed, can be replaced. The chief consideration is reproduction cost. Labor and materials may have doubled or tripled but a 1000% increase in reproduction costs could never occur except under runaway and uncontrolled inflation.

---

Land values increase as community services are made available. Police and fire protection; telephone, water, gas and electric services; churches, libraries, schools, hospitals and character building institutions all tend to increase land values. These are socially created services and their presence in the community causes increases in land values.

Building values are not affected by the multiplicity of community services available. Socially-created services that vastly improve the life style of area residents never affect the price of buildings. Reproduction costs and depreciation factors are the major considerations. The citation of a building as an historical landmark might add to its value but this rarely occurs.

---

Land worth or value is determined by a process of open market bidding. Land is worth the most that anyone at any time is willing to pay for rent or purchase. If no bids are being made, a research study of land sales in the surrounding area will serve as a useful guide.

Building values are ascertained by fairly reliable calculations, taking into account reproduction costs and standard obsolescence factors. Bids may be affected if a building is designed to meet a particular need or if alterations will be needed for the intended use.

---

*Rent* is paid for the use of land or landsites. Any increase in the tax on land value does not affect the rent payment. It does decrease the rent-take by the landowner. If the state takes 10% of the annual rent in taxes the landowner keeps 90%. If the state takes 90% the landowner keeps 10%. He cannot add to the rent to recoup the tax because he is already getting as much as the market allows. If a higher tax on land value is levied the tax on buildings should be proportionately reduced. Most of the people who own land and who use their land would benefit.

*Interest* is paid for the use of buildings. We mistakenly refer to it as rent. Inasmuch as all taxes levied on labor products will be passed on, the building owner must pay the tax if he is using the building. If he rents or sells, the user or buyer must pay. A tax levy of from 2% to 5% of the annual interest earning of the building must be paid by the user and this automatically reduces the annual earning capacity of the investment. Owners, if renting, can pass the tax on; but whether paid by owner or renter, it is the user who pays in the end.

---

A tax on land value is never punitive. It is a payment in lieu of rent. All land that is worth using calls for a rent commensurate with its value. If the rent is paid to the state as a tax, the private landowner may feel punished; but upon thinking it through, he will realize that the government is forbidding him to take what is not rightfully his. This is a legitimate function of government.

A tax on buildings is always punitive. It is an arbitirary "fine" imposed by the state and constitutes an annually collected penalty for producing or buying something of value. Such a policy is contrary to the fundamental purpose of government which should encourage and not penalize citizens for creating wealth. Every penny of taxation on buildings makes buildings more expensive.

---

Taxes on land value should never exceed the annual rental value of land or even be so high as to impair the incentive to own land or to make land deals. Landowners, as such, may do no work, but understanding and good judgment are important. For exercising such, recompense is due. If land value taxes are increased beyond a certain point, there might be no profit at all in buying or selling land. Landowners should receive reasonable remuneration; but with the risk factor removed there would be no excessive gain nor crippling loss.

Taxes on buildings should never even approach the point where the tax is so high as to impair the incentives for investment building. All over America private enterprise is being shackled because taxes are taking too much of the annual investment earning of capital. It is absurd to assume that there is enough tax money to replace all the outworn buildings, either in cities or in the country districts. By taxing land value to its full potential and taking taxes off buildings, the price of both land and buildings would be greatly reduced.

In commenting upon these basic differences let us summarize their significance:

Whereas: land is the natural God-given source of all wealth, having required no expenditure of either capital or labor; and conversely, buildings are man-made and cannot be produced without the expenditure of labor and capital—

Whereas: land values increase, due to population pressure and increased demand for raw materials, sometimes advancing thousands of percentage points beyond what they once were; and conversely, building values never increase as a result of population pressure or increased social demands upon materials, but rather are determined by obsolescence factors and reproduction costs—

Whereas: land, when taxed, becomes less expensive to buy; and conversely, buildings, when taxed, become more expensive both to build and to maintain (raw materials must be secured from high priced land, and higher taxes are necessarily paid by the user)—

Whereas: a low tax on land value makes land more expensive to buy; and conversely, a low tax on buildings, when coupled with a high tax on land value, makes buildings cheaper, both to build and maintain—

Whereas: a high tax on land value does not impair the productive capacity of land; and conversely, a high tax on buildings will result, sometimes in the razing of a building to escape the tax, but more often, in creating conditions that make the construction of buildings unprofitable, thus adding to decay and obsolescence in a city—

Whereas: all of the above is true, and it is customary to conclude such a list of "reasons why" with a solemn "let us therefore, firmly resolve," our present state of ignorance regarding property taxes prompts us to change the usual phrase to "let us, therefore, try to understand."

Let us, therefore, try to understand that: 1) it is unscientific to tax land and buildings alike; 2) any tax based upon the value of buildings and improvements will penalize builders and do-ers and thus discourage the whole building process; 3) theoretically, the only tax that can be justified is a tax based upon land value; and 4) the problems involved in clearing away the tangled growths of legal terminology embedded in federal and state constitutions will require the best of legal talent.

This could not be done all at once. It will have to be applied gradually with an agreed upon schedule, whereby taxes on land value are increased as taxes on buildings are decreased proportionately. We cannot long postpone such action, nor can we take too much time to eliminate all taxes on buildings. Unless it is done soon the cities of America will continue to develop insoluble problems beyond the ability of any individual or political party to resolve.



Author/Publisher - Wylie Young
409 Harvard Avenue
Swarthmore, Penna. 19081

TWO PARAGRAPHS FROM

CHAPTER EIGHT

# So What Good Would That Do?

Let us list briefly some of the things that would happen if we were to adopt total and complete land value taxation. They would not happen instantaneously. It would take time, but within five years after its adoption this country would be a showcase for the rest of the world to ponder. One thing *would* happen instantaneously. If it could be done rapidly, everyone would be able to find work and that in itself would serve to breathe life and hope into our shattered dreams of what America ought to be. Relief programs already in existence need not be rescinded until it became obvious that they were no longer needed. The people could be encouraged to "hang in there" until the real benefits were being developed by the application of all kinds of labor to all kinds of land.

When full and complete LVTaxation had become a reality these are some of the things that would certainly occur. Roughly, we would estimate that at least 80% of all homeowners would enjoy substantial tax reductions. 2) About 95% of all manufacturing plants would also enjoy large tax reductions, and these could encourage employment and reduce the prices of their goods. 3) A building boom would ensue as new houses could be built tax free on land that had been reduced in price. 4) Vacant areas in cities would be improved. 5) Every family would reconsider where and how it might now afford to live, and many would plan to move up to better land areas. 6) That extensive area of blight that now marks the section adjacent to the central city and extending out, sometimes as far as five miles, would begin to be rebuilt. (Clevelanders may think of Superior and St. Clair Avenues out as far as the University; Buffalonians may think of those one hundred year old buildings all around the downtown area; Philadelphians may think of those *dozens of square miles* of row houses visible on both sides of the elevated both west and north of the central city; Chicagoans may think of those terrible buildings along the elevated tracks in all directions toward the suburbs.) Every city in America has its centers of decay and all of these would vanish within a period of five or ten years. 7) All American cities are losing substantial taxpayers who are fleeing to the suburbs. This migration can be quickly reversed as new and attractive apartments are erected so that thousands can walk to their places of employment. 8) Owners of old buildings, now being abandoned, could tear them down and build fine rentable buildings in their places.

We predict that if ever the American people come to their senses and quit